Śrī Chakra Navāvarṇam
(Marvels of *Śrī Chakra*)

*

Dr. Ramamurthy N.
M.Sc., B.G.L., CAIIB, CCP, DSADP, CISA, PMP, CGBL, Ph.D.

*

*

Title:	***Śrī Chakra Navāvarṇam*** (Marvels of *Śrī* Chakra)
First Edition:	2019
Author:	**Dr. Ramamurthy N,** http://ramamurthy.jaagruti.co.in/
Copyright ©:	With the author (No part of this book may be reproduced in any manner whatsoever without the written permission from the author).
Number of pages:	141
ISBN (13):	978-93-82237-59-4

*****

Table of Contents

*****

Dedication

Śrī Mātre Nama:
Mātru Devo Bhava

This book is dedicated with devotion to all the *Śrī Vidyā Upāsakas*. All the readers of this book will be blessed with the complete compassion of *Śrī Devī*. There is not even an iota of doubt in this.

Dr. Ramamurthy N

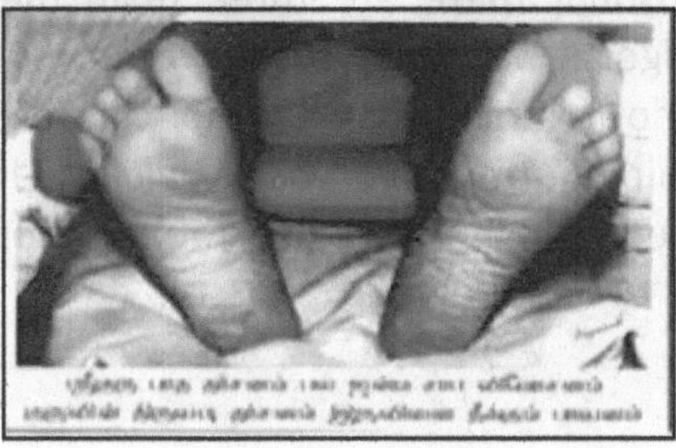

Śrī Mātre Nama:

*****

Blessings

Everyone born in this world have debts to repay to Sages, Ancestors and *Devas*. By performing *panca yagna*s (5 tasks) the human beings try to repay the debts and get punya and reach the four necessities viz. righteousness, wealth, happiness and liberation. This is the way prescribed by the holy sages.

In this regard, *upāsanā* path is the one to repay the debts to *Devas* and obtain every type of wealth. More specifically the *Śrīvidyā* path can be followed only when if the person has done some *punya* in the previous births. This has been confirmed by sages.

"Mokśaika Hetu Vidyā Sā Śrī Vidyā Eva Na Samśaya:"

Initial part of *Śrī Lalitā Trishatī*

Śrīvidyā is the only path to reach the liberation. There is no doubt in this.

Through *Śrīvidyā Upāsanā* one gets clarity in his mind, experience the truth in *Vedānta*. In this era of 'kali,' *Śrīvidyā Upāsanā* is the only one great tool to obtain all the pleasures of this and the other world.

In that *Śrīvidyā Upāsanā*, there are three main methods have been recommended by sages – *Śuddha* worship, *Mārga* worship and *Koula* worship. There is no restrictions on who can do this *Upāsanā* – irrespective of Brahmins, *Śatriyas*, *Vysyas* or *Velālas*. The right to perform this *Upāsanā* is given to all. However, the method initiated by an appropriate *guru* has to be followed.

Śāstras has clearly confirmed that if one has performed the *Śrīvidyā Upāsanā* for 3,336[1] times – right from *Guru Stotra* till *Śānti Stavam* as per *Śrīvidyā Saparya krama pūja*, then he becomes a *Śiva Yogi*.

If we deeply think over, our body itself is *Śrī Cakra* – enabling us to realise the same is the *Śrīvidyā Upāsanā*. Sages have prescribed us the method of *Navāvarṇa pūja*. By performing this *Navāvarṇa puja*, not only the worshipper gets benefitted, but also the entire world – "*Jagat yagnena truptatu*".

I am happy to note and understand that Dr. **Ramamurthy** had come out with a book detailing such a great *puja*, its benefits, lots of details about in and around *Śrī Cakra*, *Sapta Mātas*, *Titi Nityā Devī*s and so on. Also the book is written in such a smooth flow using simple language so that anyone can understand the subject very easily. Let everyone read this book and comprehend the subject. Let the readers reach an appropriate guru, get initiated ino *Śrīvidyā*. I wish the devotees to lead a happy and peaceful life by getting the blessings of the almighty *Śrīvidyā Lalitā Mahātripura Sundarī Parā Ṣoḍaśī*.

My complete blessings to Dr. **Ramamurthy**, who compiled this glorious work, his family and all the readers.

Always in the service of *Śrīdevī*
Jaya Jaya Jagadambā – Śrīgurudevadattā

Ayyarmalai   *Śrī Praṇavānunda Saraswati Swāmi*
February 2019   *Śrī Vidyā Parāmbikā Trust*

Bliss   Happyness   Auspiciousness

P.S. The blessings were given by *Swāmijī* in Tamil and translated into English by the author.

---

[1] What is the significance of the number 3,336? There are 30 *kāṇḍas* in the *Śrīvidyā Saparya krama pūja* and hence we get 3,336 x 30 = 1,00,080.

Introduction

श्री गुरुभ्यो नम: | *Śrī Gurubhyo Nama:* |

गुरुर्ब्रह्मा गुरुर्विष्णु गुरुर्देवो महेश्वर: | गुरुरेव परं ब्रह्म तस्मै श्रीगुरवे नम: ||

Gurur Brahma Gurur Viṣṇu: Gurur Devo Maheśvara: |
Gurureva Param Brahma Tasmai Śrī Gurave Nama: ||

सदाशिव सामारंभां शङ्कराचार्य मध्यमां | अस्मद आचार्य पर्यन्तां वन्दे गुरु परंपराम् ||

Sadāśiva Samārambhām Śaṅkarācārya Madhyamām |
Asmad Ācārya Paryantām Vande Guru Paramparām ||

अपार करुणा सिन्धुं ज्ञानदं शान्त रूपिणम् | श्री चन्द्रशेखर गुरु प्रणमामि मुदान्वहम् ||

Apāra Karuṇa Sindhum Gjānadam Śānta Rūpiṇam |
Śrī Candraśekhara Gurum Praṇamāmi Mudānvaham ||

वक्रतुण्ड महाकाय सूर्यकोटि समप्रभा | निर्विघ्नं कुरु मे देव सर्वकार्येषु सर्वदा ||

Vakratuṇḍa Mahākāya Sūryakoti Samaprabhā |
Nirvighnam Kuru Me Deva Sarvakāryeṣu Sarvadā ||

ज्ञानानन्दमयं देवं निर्मल स्फटिकाकृतिम् | आधारं सर्व विद्द्यानां हयग्रीवं उपास्महे ||

Gnānānandamayam Devam Nirmala Sphaṭikākrutim |
Ādhāram Sarva Viddyānām Hayagrīvam Upāsmahe ||

सरस्वति नमस्तुभ्यं वरदे कामरूपिणि | विद्यारम्भं करिष्यामि सिद्धिर्भवतु मे सदा ||

Sarasvati Namastubhyam Varade Kāmarūpiṇi |
Vidyārambham Kariṣyāmi Siddhirbhavatu Me Sadā ||

वागर्थाविव सम्पृक्तौ वागर्थ प्रतिपत्तये | जगत: पितरौ वन्दे पार्वती परमेश्वरौ ||

Vāgarthāviva Sampruktou Vāgartha Pratipattaye |
Jagata: Pitarou Vande Pārvatī Parameśvarou ||

श्रुति स्मृति पुराणानामालयं करुणालयम् | नमामि भगवत्पादंशंकरं लोकशंकरम् ||

Śruti Smruti Purāṇānāmālayam Karuṇālayam |
Namāmi Bhagavatpādam Śaṅkaram Loka Śaṅkaram ||

या देवी सर्व भूतेषु बुद्धि रूपेण संस्तिता |
नमस्तस्यै || नमस्तस्यै || नमस्तस्यै नमो नम: ||

Yā Devī Sarva Bhūteṣu Buddhi Rūpeṇa Samstitā |
Namastasyai || Namastasyai || Namastasyai Namo Nama: ||

Avanarulāle Avan Tāl Vaṇaṅgi – Bowing to all the teachers, (*gurus*) family deities and all other Gods, it is a little effort to share the knowledge obtained by us to all others also.

The author of this book, earlier wrote one book in English titled "Power of *Śrī Vidyā*" detailing the glory of *Śrī Vidyā* and another book also in English, titled "*Śrī Chakra* – An Esoteric Approach (Mathematical Construction to draw *Śrī Chakra*) [2] " detailing the mathematical construction to draw **Śrī** *Chakra*. These two books were globally well received. Based on these books, lots of doubts/ clarifications were sought over e-mail/ phone/ in person. To the possible extent there were cleared.

This book is tried at the request various readers. Such matters are available through internet or through other elders. However, 10 different persons will provide 11 different ideas and the audience will get confused. Hence an attempt has been made to provide the details authentically, with evidences, after confirming with the experts in those areas.

What a forethought Tiruvallur had – to write two *kurals*, about 2000+ years ago, anticipating our present-day knowledge through internet;

Epporul Yār Yār Vāi Ketpinum Apporul Meiporul Kāṇpatu Arivu.
Epporul Ettanmaithāyinum Apporul Meiporul Kāṇpatu Arivu.

In the words of *Kāñchi Paramācārya* – *Śrī Devī*, displays herself in physical form exclusively for people like us. She takes different holy forms in different places – **She** is;

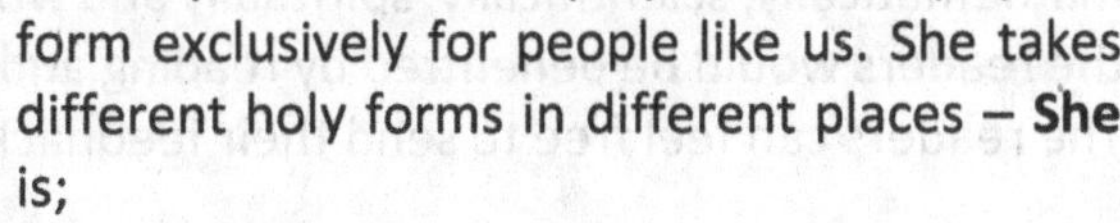

- Daughter of Parvata king at Himachal
- *Kanyākumāri* in the South end
- *Bhagavati* in Kerala
- *Cāmuṇdeśvari* in Karnataka
- *Kāmākṣi* in Tamil Nadu Tonda region
- *Akilāndeśvari* in Chola region
- *Mīnākṣi* in Pāndya region

---

[2] The entire list of books penned by this author is given at the end.

- *Gnānāmba* in Andhra
- *Tulajā Bhavāni* in Maharashtra
- *Ambāji* in Gujarat
- *Jvālāmukhī* in Punjab
- *Kṣīra Bhavāni* in Kashmir
- *Vindhyā Vāsinī* in Uttar Pradesh
- *Kāli* in Bengal
- *Kāmāgyā* in Assam

However, it is that one *Śrī Devī*, who blesses us all, seems to be, in this fashion, different forms and different names in various places across the country.

She also shines in a subtle form in *Śrī Chakra* or *Meru* or *Arddha Meru*. Let **her** be in any form. If a devotee, worships as per *Śrī Vidyā* methods, she compassionately ready to shower infinite quantum of graceful blessings. *Śrī Vidyā mantras* are very secretive. Hence, they are to be learned from an appropriate *guru*. It can be noted that it has been mentioned as "appropriate *guru*" and not simply *guru*. Because lot many persons proclaim himself as *Śrī Vidyā guru*. Nothing can be told about those persons. *Śrī Devī* has to take care. For those, who got initiated from an appropriate *guru*, this book is intended to supplement or compliment or augment the knowledge and understanding of the *japa* or *pooja* processes. Once the knowledge is expanded the results of the worship will multiply itself. *Śrī Chakra* is approached in different angles – mathematically, scientifically, spiritually and worshipping methods. Hope the readers would be benefitted by reading and understanding this book. The readers can feel free to send their feedback about the contents.

The only goal of this book is to explain about *Śrī Chakra* – around it and its nuances. In this process, some of the *mantras* had to be quoted. They are not intended for the readers to perform *japa* or *pooja* with these mantras unless otherwise taught by an appropriate *guru*. It is not the intention of this book to explain the pooja methods. They have to be got initiated from the *guru*.

Conventions; Translating and translitering Samskruta words in English is very difficult. To get an appropriate diction, most of the mantras are written in Samskrutam also. While translitering into English, diacritical marks are used for proper pronunciation and also written in *italics*. Where she/ her denotes *Śrī Devī*, it is written in bold as **She/ her**. Hope these all will help the readers.

Our sincere thanks are due to all those who helped in bringing up this book, in this form in your hands.

Our humble *pranāms* are due to HH Pranavanunda Swamijee, who blessed the author to write this book[3] and have given the blessings about the author and some small notes about the book. He is *Caṇḍi* personified – he breaths and lives *Caṇḍi*. By thinking of him, we think of the *Śrī Devī* Herself. There is no doubt that all the readers are worthy of infinite graces of *Ādhi Parāśakti*, *Paradevata*, *Śrī Lalitā Devī*.

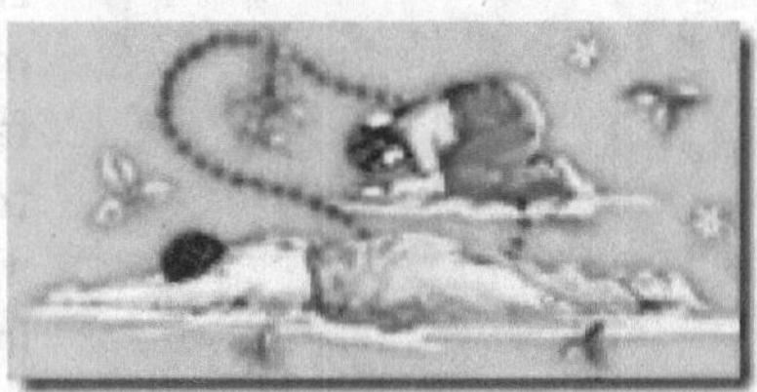

Guru Caraṇāravindābhyām Nama:

Om Tat Sat

Chennai
March 2019   *Dr. Ramamurthy N.*

*****

---

[3] The same author has written the same book in Tamil also simultaneously.

Glory of *Śrī Vidyā*

In the first part of *Śrī Lalitā Trishatī*, it has been mentioned as "*Mokśaika Hetu Vidyā Sā Śrī Vidyā Eva Na Samśaya:*". The only way to liberation (*mokśam*) is *Śrī Vidyā*. There can be no doubt in this.

Lord *Parameśvara* has blessed us all various *Vedas, Śāstras, Smrutis, Purāṇās, Itihāsas*, etc., to reach the eternal liberation. These depend on the devotee and his clarity of mind. *Śrī Ādhi Śaṅkarar* in his *Soundaryalaharī*, 31st verse, explains that *Parameśvara*, after providing all the *Tantra Śāstras* to this world, at the behest of *Śrī Devī*, blessed the world with *Śrī Tantra*, which is the gist of all the *Tantra Śāstras*. This has got the special name called *Śrīpura Upāsanā or Śrī Vidyā*[4].

Worship (*Vidyā*) of *Devī*, who is denoted by the letter '*Śrī*' is *Śrī Vidyā*. The Samskruta letter '*Śrī*' has lots of meanings – particular meaning is wealth. In general, it means goddess *Lakśmī Devī*. Since everyone is behind money/ wealth, this worship is world famous. However, *Śrī Vidyā* is a path to worship Goddess *Durgā*. *Śrī Vidyā* means knowledge of *Śrī Devī*, most important acquaintance or real path leading to liberation. This complicated, traditional worship will lead to adoration to various other Gods. *Śrī Chakra* or its highest form *Mahā Meru* is a representation of development in this regard.

The aim of the worship method called *Śrī Vidyā* is – realizing through experiences that self and *Parabrahmam* are one the same – this is what the *Vedānta Mahā* sentences communicate.

---

[4] 585th name in *Śrī Lalitā Sahasranāma* is just *Śrī Vidyā*. It affirms that *Śrī Lalitā Devī* is *Śrī Vidyā* and *Śrī Vidyā* is *Śrī Lalitā Devī*.

Kāñchi Paramācārya, who is considered as an incarnation of *Ādhi Śaṅkara*, has clearly explained in detail that *Brahma Vidyā* and *Śrī Vidyā* are one and the same (Voice of God volume 6). *Śrī Vidyā* is an ancient and most influential *Śākta tantra*. *Śrī Vidyā* can be majorly classified into three;

- Worshipping *Śrī Lalitā Tripurasundarī*
- **Her** *mantras*
- **Her** *yantra* called *Śrī Chakra*

Śrī Vidyā is composed of a systematic, orderly scheme that combines elements of perception, devotion and *yoga*. In the *Śrī Vidyā* tradition, *Śrī Chakram* is a *Yantra* (symbolic figure) for worship. When it is raised to a 3-dimensional figure, it becomes '*Meru*'. Actually, the top angle view of *Meru* is the *Śrī Chakram*.

In *Śrī Chakram*, the journey from the exterior *Bhūpuram* till the central *Bindu* in a step by step path to one's own journey to reach the *Brahmam*. This ritual practice is known as the "*Navāvarṇa Pūja*". *Āvarṇa* can mean a curtain, screen, block, fence, wall, fort, etc. However, in this context we can take it as enclosures located one by one. In fact, a devotee gradually crossing every *āvarṇa* and reaching/ connecting with the divine mother is, in practice, one by one removing the curtains of ignorance.

Each of the *āvarṇa* is dedicated to a particular God. There are Gods and hand signs (*Mudras*) pertaining to every stage of *Śrī Chakra*. When a devotee moves to next *āvarṇa* he is raised one step. The travel from the outer *Bhūpuram* till inner *Bindu* is, the awakening of man's dominant power – the *Kundalinī* energy sleeping in *Mūlādhāra* raises and surprisingly unifying with the *Brahmam* by reaching the *Sahasrāra*.

<u>Worshipping *Śrī Chakra*</u>;

It has been mentioned in the book called "*Lalitopākyānam*" as;

Kāmākṣyeva Mahālakṣmī: Chakram Śrī Chakrameva Ca |
Śrī Vidyaiva Parāvidyā…….

Only *Kāmākṣī* is *Mahālakśmī*. *Chakram* means it is *Śrī Chakram* and *Parāvidyā* is *Śrī Vidyā*. Worshipping of *Śrī Chakram* can be done as outward rituals (*Bahirmukha*[5]) in a common place like a temple for the welfare of the society as a whole. The procedures recommended in this regard are very labourious, but still a person can do it to the extent possible (*yatāśakti*). Or it can also be through inward rituals (*Antarmukha*[6]) in a house for the welfare of self and/ or the family. It is worshiped with its symbols through the *Mantras* and *Dyānas*.

The highest form of *Śrī Vidyā* is worshipping *Śrī Chakra* or *Meru* is *Navāvarṇa* worship. Such a worship takes the devotee to *Śrīpuram*, by raising his sub-conscious carries itself to the body, self-recognition or illumination of the body. The devotee modifies his body itself as a place of worship. He burns it, by sacrificing the same, in the holy fire. By the grace of Lord *Śiva* and *Śakti* he gets back his body. He imagines himself as a female to worship the divine mother. The path travelled by the *Kundalinī* from *Mūlādhāra* till *Sahasrāra*, is the same the devotee travelling from *Bhūpuram* till *Bindu* in the *Navāvarṇa* worship, through the nine *āvarṇas*. It is similar to the unison of *Śiva* and *Śakti*. *Śiva* and *Śakti* are not different from *Parabrahmam*. It is there in the body of every human being. Our body is *Piṇḍāṇdam* and the universe is the *Aṇḍāṇdam*. Realizing that both *Piṇḍāṇdam* and the *Aṇḍāṇdam* are one and the same is *Advaitam* (no two).

Lastly, the celebrant's body itself, during worshipping, is assumed as an embodiment of a temple dwelled by *Śrī Devī* herself. This is the highest maturity stage of *Śrī Vidyā*. Any ritual done, without understanding the inherent philosophies is a wasteful exercise. It has been compared to a donkey loaded with the sandal woods does not know the significance of sandal – neither know the difference between a thorn wood and a sandal

---

[5] 871st name in *Śrī Lalitā Sahasranāma* – *Bahirmukha Sudurlabhā* – बहिर्मुखसुदुर्लभा

[6] 870th name in *Śrī Lalitā Sahasranāma* – *Antarmukha Samārādhyā* – अन्तर्मुखसमाराध्या

wood. It is the fate of the donkey. Same way it is the fate of the worshipper. Hence it is imperative, for the worshipper to comprehend the inherent importance behind the traditional rituals and then follow the same. Then only he gets the complete benefit of them. *Śrī Chakra* worship is a spectacular tool of this universe, for stimulating our mind and spiritually develop self and our ancient *sanātana dharma*. Hence, the *Pañcadaśākśarī* and *Ṣoḍaśākśarī mantras* are initiated only to those disciples, who completely surrender with the *guru*.

The worship and the worshipper

Those who worship *Śakti* are called *Śāktas*. Those who do *Śrī Vidyā* pooja are called *Upāsakas*. *Mantra, yantra* and *tantra* are the three vertices of the *Śrī Vidyā* triangle. The *mantra* is displayed in the *yantra*. The inward or outward *pooja* in a *yantra* is practically depend on the performance of performer and his capacity. The main *mantra* of *Śrī Vidyā* is the *Pañcadaśākśarī*. The main *yantra* of *Śrī Vidyā* is the *Śrī Chakra*. The key part of it is that *Śrī Devī* herself is iconized in the *tantra, mantra* and *yantras*. The *Śrī Vidyā* worship has to be performed with focused mind, appreciation and kindness in the heart. In that case, the *mantras, yantras,* offering, the pooja process and the disciplines are all converted into the expressions of *Chit-Śakti* form. The inherent philosophy is to transform the contents and the ordinary experiences into the bliss of the divine mother.

Soudaryalaharī affirms – If someone is subtly committed to heart and perform the worship – his ordinary speech becomes *japam*, the normal work of his hands becomes signets, his general walking becomes circum-ambulation (*pradakśinam*), taking food is offering in a holy fire and normal lying down becomes bowing. That is, what the person naturally does is converted into a worship. He need not separately do anything.

Only a male or a couple (husband and wife) are eligible to do most of the *karmas* prescribed in *Vedas*. But, *Śrī Vidyā* is an exception. It can be followed by any one at any time – irrespective of caste, creed, sex, etc. Śrī Krishna himself says in Gītā (9-32);

"Striyo vaiśyā: tatā sūdrā: tespi yānti parām gatim|"

However, some rules like dos and don'ts are prescribed for the worshippers of *Śrī Vidyā*.

"Na Śaḍāya Na Duṣṭāya Nā Viṣvāsāya Garhicit |"

The *gurus* have been cautioned by *Śāstras*, not to initiated, immoral persons, characterless (blackguards) persons and those who do not have confidence on *Śrī Vidyā*.

It has been mentioned that the *upāsakas* of *Śrī Vidyā* have to follow some rules. The worshipper should;

- Not talk ill or wrong of other *upāsana* methods
- Always do *japa* in the background.
- Not demand offerings neither accept from others.
- Continue to do his duties properly
- Worship God, without expecting any fruits.
- Be fearless
- Not accept wealth and money with a selfish intention.
- Should not consider anything above than self-realization
- Importantly should not be revealing that he is *Śrī Vidyā upāsaka*. *Śrī Vidyā upāsana* is very secretive and the secrecy should always be maintained.

Stages of *Śrī Vidyā* – There are many steps in the ladder of *Śrī Vidyā*;

- Frist stage – *Mahā Gaṇapati upāsana* – in the *Śrī Vidyā* tradition *Gaṇapati* is called as "*Śrī Vidyā Mahā Vallabha Gaṇapati*". This is to get rid of all the obstrucles.
- Next is *Mahā Śyāmalā* called as *Mantrinī upāsana*. This is to get good intelligence. This *mahā mantra* has 98 letters. A book called "*Matanga Manukoṣam*" says that once this mantra is obtained, all other mantras can be got, just by going through once.
- Next in the sequence in *Vārāhi upāsana* – a person who is successful in his life should realize that the basis for the entire cosmos. Getting that cosmic consciousness is the goal of *Vārāhi upāsana*.
- Next is an important stage in *Śrī Vidyā* – *Bālā upāsana* – *Tripura Rahasya* says "*Bālā Līlā Viśiṣtatvād Bāleti Gatitāpriye*". *Paradevata* loves to play like a little girl and hence this name. This mantra is also

called as *Laghu Śrī Vidyā mantra*. The word *Laghu* in Samskrutam has two meanings – easy and brief. Both the senses befit here.

- The three lettered (*Trayakṣara*[7]) *mantra* of *Bālā Tripura Sundarī* gets expanded to the next stage called *Mahā Pañcadaśākśarī mantra*
- And to the next stage *Śrī Ṣoḍaśākśarī mantra*.

Two different paths are there in *Śrī Vidyā upāsana* – *Koula mārga* and *Samaya mārga*. *Samaya mārga* again has two variations – *Dakśiṇācāra* and *Vāmācāra*. Each of these two various has three sub-sections called *Bāhyā* (*Aparā*), *Āndra* (*Parā*) and *Parāparā* (both mixed).

Śrī Vidyā						
Samaya mārga [8]						Koula mārga [9]
Dakśiṇācāra			Vāmācāra			
Bāhyā	Āndra	Parāparā	Bāhyā	Āndra	Parāparā	

Clearly understanding *Śrī Vidyā upāsana* in the above routes/ stages will lead to satisfaction and fulfilment for the different and sometimes contradicting minds of the human beings.

A well-known great person Ramakrishna Paramahamsa authoritatively confirms – one real *Śrī Vidyā upāsakar* can only be real *Śāktar*. He can also be *Śaivite* outside, *Vaiṣṇavaite* in practice. Such a reconciliation is possible. He has proved that all the paths, once followed with devotion leads to the same single God. The *mantras* are definitely rewarding. *Yantras* are surely powerful. There are definitely gods and high powers.

---

[7] 630th name in *Śrī Lalitā Sahasranāma* – *Trayakśarī* – त्र्यक्षरी

[8] 98th name in *Śrī Lalitā Sahasranāma* – *Samayācāratatparā* – समयाचारतत्परा

[9] 441st name in *Śrī Lalitā Sahasranāma* – *Koulamārgatatparasevitā* – कौलमार्गतत्परसेविता

Siddhis can be achieved. The benefit of worship of the divine mother, gradually elevates in the right path till the goal is reached.

Tantras say – following the *Śrī Vidyā upāsana* without mental maturity or without proper guidance from an appropriate *guru*, is like walking on the edge of a sword. It is like hugging the neck of a tiger – like hanging a snake in the neck. Such a danger may happen.

Śrī Vidyā is not something, which everyone can get. This is the only path/ tool to liberation. For whomsoever, this is the last birth or who is in the form Śaṅkara he only will be fortunate to get initiated in *Śrī Vidyā*.

*****

The Philosophy of *Pañcadaśākśarī Mantra*

Sages have advised worshipping *Śrī Devī* in four different methods;

1. Physical (*Stūla tama*) form – The form created by the sculptures with his expertise. This can be in Gold, Silver, Copper, Five-metals or stone.
2. Physical (*Stūla tara*) form – *Śrī Devī* in scripted through lines like *Śrī Chakra*. We have such *Chakras* for most of other Gods also.
3. Physical (*Stūla*) form – imaging the form of Gods, in particular, *Śrī Devī* in the heart.
4. Subtle (*Stūla*) form – Worshipping *Śrī Devī* in the form of *mantras*. "*Mannāt Drāyate Iti Mantra:*" – that which protects the chanter is *mantra*.

Among the above, the last one – Worshipping *Śrī Devī* in the subtle (*Stūla*) form is *Pañcadaśākśarī manta*.

The 32nd verse of Soundaryalaharī;

शिव: शक्ति: काम: क्षिति–रथ रवि: शीतकिरण: स्मरो हंस: शक्र–स्तदनु च परा–मार–हरय: ।
अमी हृल्लेखाभि–स्तिसृभि–रवसानेषु घटिता भजन्ते वर्णास्ते तव जननि नामावयवताम् ॥

Śiva: Śakti: Kāma: Kśiti-ratha Ravi: Śītakiraṇa:
Smaro Hamsa: Śakra-stadanu Ca Parā-māra-haraya: |
Amī Hrllīkhābhi-stisrubhi-ravasāneṣu Ghaṭitā
Bhajante Varṇāste Tava Janani Nāmāvayavatām ||

The above verse explains the gist of *Śrī Vidyā Pañcadaśākśarī mantra*;

Among the *Śrī Vidyā upāsakas* there are 12 major *upāsakas*. They are called mantra *Draṣṭas* – who got the mantras in their mind (eyes), they did not learn from anyone and hence this name. They are – *Manu, Candra* (Moon), *Kubera, Lopāmudrā* wife of sage *Agastya, Manmada* (Cupid), Sage *Agastya, Agni, Sūriya* (Sun), *Indra, Skanda, Paramaśiva* and sage *Durvāsa*.

Each of the above 12, have preached *Pañcadaśākṣarī mantras*. Among them only two are presently available and known – *Khādhi Vidyā* preached by *Manmada* and *Hādhi Vidyā* preached by *Lopāmudrā*[10].

Śrī Lalitā Sahasranāma, Śrī Lalitā Triśatī, Mahā Śoḍaśī mantra, etc., are all based on *Khādhi Vidyā* only.

Our divine mother *Śrī Devī* is in the form of *Pañcadaśākṣarī mantra* obtained by adding the *Śākta praṇava mantra* 'Hrīm (ह्रीं)[11]' to the below letters[12];

1. '*Ka* (क)' – the root letter (*Bījākṣaram*) of *Śiva*.
2. '*E* (ए)' – the root letter (*Bījākṣaram*) of *Śakti*.
3. '*Ī* (ई)' – the root letter (*Bījākṣaram*) of *Manmada* (Cupid), the God of love.
4. '*La* (ल)' – the root letter (*Bījākṣaram*) of *Goddess Earth*.
5. '*Ha* (ह)' – the root letter (*Bījākṣaram*) of Sun.
6. '*Sa* (स)' – the root letter (*Bījākṣaram*) of Moon with cool rays.

We are aware that *Pañcadaśākṣarī mantra* has 15 letters. Calculating 20 names for each of 15 letters - 15 x 20 = 300, names have been advised in *Śrī Lalitā Triśatī*[13]. That is, *Śrī Lalitā Triśatī*, inscribes *Pañcadaśākṣarī mantra* and hence treated as very high.

Vedas and *mantra Śāstras* describe symbolic names for letters. Based on this the names for the letters in the *Pañcadaśākṣarī mantra*;

Ka – kāma, E – yoni, Ī – kamalā, La – vajrapāṇi, Hrīm – Guhā, Ha sa – Hasā, Ka – mādariśvā, La – Indra, Hrīm – Punarguhā, Sa ka la – Sakalā, Hrīm – Māyayā and La – Indra.

This is the *Pañcadaśākṣarī mantra*, as described by sage Agastya in his book called "*Śrī Vidyā Dīpikā*".

---

[10] 647th name in *Śrī Lalitā Sahasranāma – Lopāmudrārcitā*

[11] '*Om* (ॐ)' is the *praṇava mantra* for all the *mantras*. '*Hreem* - (ह्रीं)' is the *Śākta praṇava mantra*.

[12] These letters are repeated.

[13] The author of this book has penned two books separately – the translation of *Śrī Ādhi Śaṅkara's bhāṣyam* for *Śrī Lalitā Triśatī* in English and Tamil.

Among these 15 letters;

- 2 letters pertain to *Śiva* – *Ka, Ha*
- 4 letters pertain to *Śakti* – *E, Ī, La, Sa*
- 1 letter is common *Śiva-Śakti* – *Hrīm*

Now again if we go through summary of the above Soundaryalaharī verse – it goes;

Oh Mother! '*Ka*' the root letter of *Śiva*, '*A*' the root letter of *Śakti*, '*E*' the root letter of *Manmada*, '*La*' the root letter of Earth, '*Ha*' the root letter of Sun, '*Sa*' the root letter of Moon – all these your letters added with '*Hrīm*' the letter of *Bhuvaneśvari* at the end of each *Kūṭa* (hall), become the organs of your *manta*.

There are some connections between the 15 lettered *Pañcadaśī mantra* and 24 lettered *Gāyatrī* [14]*mantra*;

#	Pañcadaśī	Gāyatrī
1.	Ka	Tat
2.	E	Savitu: Vareṇyam
3.	Ī	Bargo devasya dhī
4.	La	Mahi
5.	Hrīm	Dhiyo yo na: pracodayāt
6.	Ha	Tat
7.	Sa	Savitu:
8.	Ka	Vareṇyam Bargo devasya dhī
9.	Ha	Bargo devasya dhī
10.	La	Mahi
11.	Hrīm	Dhiyo yo na: pracodayāt
12.	Sa	Tatsavitu: Vareṇyam
13.	Ka	Bargo devasya dhī
14.	La	Mahi
15.	Hrīm	Dhiyo yo na: pracodayāt

Pañcadaśī mantra is split into three *Kūṭas*;

---

[14] 420th name in *Śrī Lalitā Sahasranāma* – *Gāyatrī*

- *Ka, E, Ī, La, Hrīm – Vāgbhava Kūṭa, Agni Kaṇḍam, Rig Veda*
- *Ha, Sa, Ka, Ha, La, Hrīm – Kāmarāja Kūṭa, Sūriya Kaṇḍam, Yajur Veda*
- *Sa, Ka, La, Hrīm – Śaktibhava Kūṭa, Candra Kaṇḍam, Sāma Veda*

In the same manner, *Gāyatrī mantra*, is also split into three *pādās* (quarters). Each *pādā* is taken from each of the *Vedas*;

- *Tat savitu: Vareṇyam –* तत्सवितुर्वरे एयं *– Rig Veda*
- *Bargo devasya dhī mahi –* भर्गो देवस्य धीमहि *– Yajur Veda*
- *Dhiyo yo na: pracodayāt –* धियो यो नः प्रचोदयात् *– Sāma Veda*

Tripuropaniṣad assures that once *Pañcadaśī japa* is equal to thrice *Gāyatrī japa*.

One caution (at the cost of repetition) – Everyone is eligible to chant *Pañcadaśī mantra* – be it male/ female or any caste or any religion. However, definitely this has to be got initiated by an appropriate *guru*. On the other hand, *Gāyatrī mantra* can be chant only by male who have been done with *Upanayana*.

<u>*Pañcadaśī* and *pancabhūtas* (five elements of nature);</u>

The five elements of nature – Ether, Air, Fire, Water and Earth, have originated from the consonants in Pañcadaśī *mantra*;

- Ether has only one character – Sound
- Air has two characters – Sound and Touching
- Fire has three characters – Sound, touching and form
- Water has four characters – Sound, touching, form and taste
- Earth has five characters – Sound, touching, form, taste and smell.

In total $1 + 2 + 3 + 4 + 5 = 15$ has to be assumed as characters of *Pañcadaśī mantra*.

<u>*Śrī Ṣoḍaśākṣarī Vidyā*</u>[15] - When the fourth one *Candra Kalā Kūṭa* with *Śrīm*, the root letter of *Ramā*, is added with *Pañcadaśī mantra*, this gets

---

[15] 587th name in *Śrī Lalitā Sahasranāma – Śrī Ṣoḍaśākṣarī Vidyā*

completed and becomes 16 lettered *Śrī Ṣoḍaśākṣarī mantra* and becomes the *Śrī Vidyā*.

Śrī Vidyā is a deep ocean of nectar. Will an ordinary man like us, be able to jump into this and take out the pearls? However, with her own blessings an attempt was made to think of **her** a little. If there are any errors "*Kṣamasva Parameśvarī*".

*****

The Structure of *Śrī Chakra*

The architecture of *Śrī Chakra* is a complicated wizard. It has a series of nine triangles along with a center point. Before we delve into the details of the structure of *Śrī Chakra*, let us know something in general about *Śrī Chakra* – definition and meaning of it;

बिंदु त्रिकोण वसु कोण दशारयुग्मं, मन्वस्र नागदल संयुत षोडशास्म् ।
वृत्तत्रयं च धरणीं सदनत्रयं च, श्री चक्रमेवमुदितं पर देवतायाः ॥

Bindu Trikoṇa Vasu Koṇa Daśārayugmam,
Manvasra Nāgadala Samyuta Ṣoḍaśāram |
Vruttatrayam Ca Dharaṇīm Sadanatrayam Ca,
Śrī Chakramevamuditam Para Devatāyā: ||

The *Śrī Chakram* belonging to the highest *Devī* (*Paradevatai*) contains, one dot, one triangle, one octagon, two decagons (ten-sided shape), one 14-sided figure, eight petals, 16 petals, three circles and on all the four sides three lined squares. The midpoint *Bindu* indicates the unison of *Śiva* and *Śakti*. A method of worshipping a *yantra* through mantras is *Śrī Chakram*.

In any worship *mantras*, *tantras* and *yantras* are used;

- <u>*Mantras*</u> – the verses used during a worship. 204th name in *Śrī Lalitā Sahasranāma* – *Sarva Mantra Rūpiṇī* again 227th name in *Śrī Lalitā Sahasranāma* – *Mahā Mantra* – these indicate that *Śrī Lalitā Devī* is in the form of *mantras*.
- <u>*Tantras*</u> – The offerings done during a pooja like camphor, food, etc. 206th name in *Śrī Lalitā Sahasranāma* – *Sarva Tantra Rūpā* again 226th name in *Śrī Lalitā Sahasranāma* – *Mahā Tantra* – these indicate that *Śrī Lalitā Devī* is in the form of *tantras*.
- <u>*Yantras*</u> – As discussed in the previous chapter, it is the *Stūla Tara* form of *Śrī Devī* – a drawing with *mantras* in the shape of a Chakra or talisman, etc., – these have three types of energies – a plate generally made of copper or five-metals. The word *yantraṇam* means "to control". Worshipping a *yantra* controls the desires like *kāma*, *krodha*, etc., – *Shaḍribuks* (six internal enemies). The yantras are equal to the Gods they represent. 205th name in *Śrī Lalitā*

Sahasranāma – Sarva Yantrātmikā again 228th name in *Śrī Lalitā Sahasranāma – Mahā Yantra –* these indicate that *Śrī Lalitā Devī* is in the form of *yantras*.

Among the herbs only some can cure some diseases. Among the words only the word of *Veda mantras* only has some potency. In this manner, only some lines drawn in a particular fashion/ design have bounteous divine power. They are the *yantras/ Chakras*. Serious devotees would like to do *pooja* in a *yantra* instead of a statute. In any pooja, the worshipper has to meditate upon self, his *guru, mantra* and the concerned deity and imagine that they are all one and the same. To make a place worthy of pooja, it has to be made ready with *mantras, tantras* and *yantras*.

Similar to *Śrī Chakra* is mapped to *Śrī Devī*, there are various *Chakras* pertaining to different Gods. When any God is installed in a temple, the corresponding *Chakra* would be placed beneath the statue. These *Chakras* emanate some vibrations, of course not feelable by human beings. Since the sanctum sanctorum is filled with these vibrations, the devotees, moving across, are cleansed, are able to concentrate on the deity and get their legal prayers satiated. It has been told that 27 such *Chakras* are kept beneath the statue of the main deity at Tirumala and hence even if a devotee passes through for a micro/ Nano second, he gets peace and happiness and all his wishes are satisfied.

A *yantra* is also called as *Chakra*. Among all the *Chakras* pertaining to various deities, *Śrī Chakra* is called as *Chakra Raja* (king of all *Chakras*). *Śrī Chakra* is also called as *Śrī Maṇḍalam*. This is considered the god of wisdom or supreme knowledge. That is *Śrī Vidyā*.

The *yantras* pertaining to most of other Gods are kept beneath or in front of the deities in temples. But with regard to *Śrī Chakra, Śrī Devī* herself is iconized in the *yantra* and worshipped. Hence this *Chakra* has a special status among the *Chakras*.

Śrī Chakra or *Śrī Yantra* is a beautiful, complex and sacred geometrical diagram used for devotion and meditation. This has been in use for 1000s of years. Its origin is not yet known to the world. It is a mathematical marvelous/ miracle. It consists of multiple inter-connected triangles meeting at particular points. That is the reason drawing[16] this figure is a very difficult task.

Śrī Chakra is a symbol of standardized movement from ancient days. *Śrī Chakra* is a;

- A device or tool. It is a go down of energy.
- This has a capacity to convert one type of energy into other one.
- The unrestricted form of omnipotence is within a controlled form
- A shape, defining unlimited measurements through lines, triangles, squares and circles.
- Indicates the dynamics of divinity.
- Transfers divine enthusiasm.

Śrī Chakra is a particular form containing different squares and triangles connected to the package in the cutting points at various edges. The word '*Śrī*' is used as a perfect adventure – a tool to make a good mind. It is a geometric representation of the cosmic energies. A complete clear description of the structure of *Śrī Chakra* has been provided in the 11th verse of Soundaryalaharī;

चतुर्भिः श्रीकण्ठैः शिवयुवतिभिः पञ्चभिरपि प्रभिन्नाभिः शम्भोर्नवभिरपि मूलप्रकृतिभिः ।

चतुश्चत्वारिंशद्वसुदल-कलाश्र-त्रिवलय- त्रिरेखाभिः सार्धं तव शरणकोणाः परिणताः ॥

Chaturbhiḥ Śrīkaṇṭhaiḥ Śivayuvatibhiḥ Pañchabhirapi
Prabhinnābhiḥ Śambhōrnavabhirapi Mūlaprakṛtibhiḥ ।
Chatuśchatvāriṃśad-Vasudala-Kalāśch-Trivalaya-
Trirēkhābhiḥ Sārdhaṃ Tava Śaraṇakōṇāḥ Pariṇatāḥ ॥

Its translation goes – these nine *Chakras* form the basis of this world with;

- Four triangles having the characters of *Śiva* (*Majjā*, *Śuklam*, *Prāṇan* and *Jīvan*)
- Five triangles having the characters of *Śakti* (*tvak*, *aśruk*, *māmsam*, *metas* and *asti*)
- *Śiva-Śakti Chakras* without touching each other

---

[16] The author of this book has drawn *Śrī Cakra* in a computer using Auto-cad and has authored a book titled "*Śrī Cakra*, An Esoteric Approach" using the computer images and explaining the mathematical construction. He has also talked about this in Internation conferences/ symposiums.

Your (*Devī's*) representation can be split into four parts;

- One eight petalled
- One 16 petalled
- One three circled
- Gapped lines in all the four sides
- Totaling 44 triangles.

Another book on *Śrī Devī*, called *Yāmalā*, describes *Śrī Chakra* in a different way – it is a shape containing one dot, triangle, hexagon, two decagons and one 14-sided figure. It has one eight petalled lotus, one 16 petalled lotus and squares around called as *Bhūpuras*. This is the *Chakra* of the uppermost *Devī*.

Let us enjoy from the talk by *Kāñchi* Paramācārya about *Śrī Chakra* (from the book "Voice of God");

The divine mother, affectionately called as '*Ambāl*' by us, has different forms like *Mīnākshī, Durgā, Bhuvaneśwarī, Śāradā* and so on. Every such form has individual *yantras*. However, thought the worshippers of *Śrī Devī* adore the different forms, in *yantra* form they all perform pooja only to Śrī *Chakra*. This is not only in houses, but also in famous temples of *Śrī Devī* – *Śāradā* is the main deity at *Śruṅgeri*, but only *Śrī Chakra* is installed and worshipped instead of the *Śāradā yantra*. In *Bhuvaneśwarī* temple at Pudukottai, the main pooja is only for *Meru* and *Bhuvaneśwarī yantra* is not used. These are evidences to show the importance of *Śrī Chakra*.

Śrī Chakra is a combination of lines, circles, squares and triangles. These are all integrated with the center point called *Bindu*. Such a design only can bring the energy pertaining to a particular deity. Actually, it is a storehouse of infinite energy. Hence, it can be called as fictional design. This design collects and accept the divine vigor. Further they have more energy to supply energy.

One *yantra* is a drawing of lines or circles or angles drawn in a prescribed measurements and ratios. There cannot be any deviation plus or minus. If a *mantra* is wrongly chant, it can result in negative impact or even end up with destruction. In the same manner, if there is an error in drawing of a *yantra*, it may end up in devastation.

If the vertex of the middle triangle in *Śrī Chakra* is kept towards West instead of East the result will be negated. Hence when a worshipper sits in front of a *Śrī Chakra* the vertex of the middle triangle should be near him and not towards opposite side. During worship of *yantras*, the worshipper has to follow the prescribed procedures/ rules more strictly than worshipping an idol. He should be more careful in this regard.

In modern days, lot many worship *Śrī Chakra* in their houses. In general, this is very good. But many do it as a pride, some do it as a style and some with ignorance. But the customs are not strictly followed. Resultantly, they suffer for want of peace.

It is not enough if one wants to follow the bigger things. Exact rules prescribed by *Śāstras* have to be clearly understood, absorbed and followed. These are time tested and handed over to us by our ancestors. It is our duty to stringently follow the same and get benefited. Definitely *Śrī Chakra* has been raised upto the sky by the *Śāstras*. But the same *Śāstras* have recommended lots of dos and don'ts, lots of processes. The approach that "I will do the pooja in my way" is not acceptable, the expected fruits will be missed. Sometimes that may result in negative angle.

One *yantra* is not a place of dwelling for the deity; It is the deity her/ himself. It is not an alternative to the deity. It is not a representation – it the deity. It is all the more apt in the case of *Śrī Devī*. Her divine presence *Śrī Chakra* is very special. That is because, importance is given to the *Yantra* than her idol.

Thus, conveys *Paramācārya*. Let us all bow his lotus feet.

*****

Parts of *Śrī Chakra*

Lord Hayagrīva, details about *Śrī Chakra* to Agastya, even before he asked about it;

Na Teṣām Siddhidā Vidyā Kalpakoṭi Śatairapi |
Caturbhi: Śiva Chakraiśca Śakti Chakraiśca Pancabhi: | |
Nava Chakraśca Samsiddham Śrī Chakram Śivayor Vapu: |
Trikoṇa Maṣṭa Koṇañca Daśakoṇa Dvayam Tatā |
Catur Daśārañcai Tāni Śakti Cakrāṇi Panca Ca | |

The *Śrī Chakra* has the following components;

- At the center the '*Bindu*', a dot. This is an embodiment of the *Brahmānanda* or Supreme bliss that is the result of the union of male and female aspects of *Brahmam*, ready to create the Universe.
- The *Trikoṇa* (the small triangle) around the *Bindu*.
- *Aṣṭakoṇa* or *Vasukoṇa* – the group of eight triangles surrounding the *Trikoṇa*.
- *Antadaśara* – the inner group of ten triangles – around the inner triangles.
- *Bahirdaśara* – the outer group of ten triangles – around the inner triangles.
- *Caturdaśara* – the fourteen triangles surrounding the *Bahirdaśara*.
- The eight-petalled lotus or *aṣtadala* around *Caturdaśara*
- The sixteen-petalled lotus encircling the *aṣtadala*.
- The three girdles like circles around the sixteen-petalled lotus.
- The *Bhūpura* – the three quadrangular lines with gate like openings on all the four sides.

Now different schools raise two questions;

1. The *Bhūpuras* or the three quadrangular compound walls-like lines – do they have a gate or opening on each of the four sides or not? In both the versions quoted above, there is no specific mention about the *Bhūpuras* having gate like openings on all the four sides. One of the commentators on *Soundaryalaharī* quotes the *Yāmalā* stanza differently. This specifies the gate like openings on all the four sides. There is a *Vedic* statement '*Śatadvārattāragamamtā*' (*Taitrīya Āranyaka* 1.31). This

clearly states that the four sides have one gate each. However, still there are quite a few schools of *Śrī Chakra* worshippers follow the closed rampart.

The *Paraśurāma Kalpa Sūtra*, which prescribes the procedures for worshipping *Śrī Chakra* emphasizes that the *Bhūpura* or the quadrangular enclosures have no openings on the sides. The commentator on the *Sūtra*, *Śrī Rāmeśwar Sūri* has written a long note on this issue and concludes that there are no openings on the four sides.

Further, another great authority, who has written an elaborate commentary on *Paraśurāma Kalpa Sūtra*, standardizing the *pooja* procedures, *Śrī Umānandanāḍa* in his book called 'Nityotsava' also, accepted the four gates. His guru *Śrī Bhāskararāya* in his book called "Sethu Bandha" has accepted the unbroken outer enclosure lines. However, the *Vedic* authority-based view is considered by the majority of worshippers.

2. Another controversial question is – how many triangles are there in *Śrī Chakra* – 43 or 44. Actually the tally of triangles is;

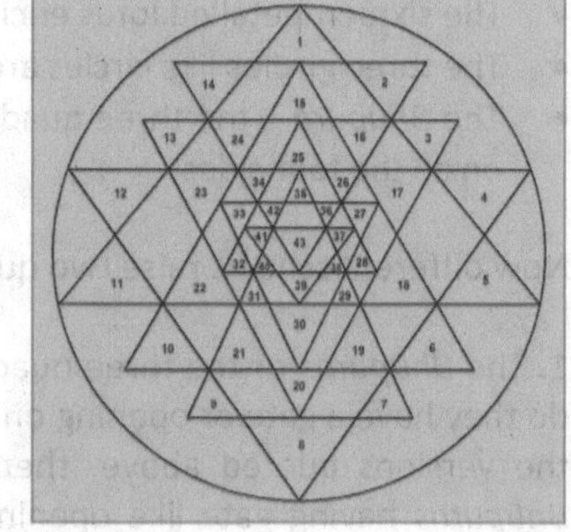

Koṇas of the *Caturdaśara* -   14
D*aśaras* of ten each 2 x 10-   20
The *Aṣṭakoṇa*   -   08
The inner triangle   -   01

Total   -   43

If the *Bindu* at the center of the inner triangle is also considered as a *kona*, then the total becomes 43 + 1 = 44. Further the three girdle-like circles are not explained anywhere, nor are they counted in the worship. However, in some parts of North India, this is also considered separately, during performing *pooja* in which case the number of *Āvaraṇas* increases. Some schools consider the *Bindu* at the center as a triangle. But in reality, it is a circle – more specifically a dot. Mathematically, a dot is considered as a smallest possible circle, that is, with '0' radius. A circle has no starting point, neither an end – neither *ādhi* nor *antam*. That is *Bindu*.

The mathematical shapes in *Śrī Chakra* has some deep philosophies;

- Circle – None can identify the beginning nor the end. This indicates the divinity, which does not have a birth nor an end.
- Triangle – Any triplets like – creation, maintenance and destruction – satva, *rajas* and *tamas* and so on. These triple energies are the three vertices of a triangle. The upward triangle indicates high goal. If it is downward it indicates the feature of a *Śakti*. One triangle being upward and the other downward – being a hexagon – indicate high goal and refers the lord coming towards the devotee.
- Lotus petals – Lotus blooms when Sun rises and closes when Sun sets. The lotus petals in *Śrī Chakra* indicates the blooming inner energy of the devotee. When it closes, the worshippers mind also concentrates on the deity.
- Square – The squares in a *Śrī Chakra* encloses all the shapes. The powers, energies and the meanings are controlled so that they do not spill over. Only in a controlled environment the required wishes are satiated.

There are various *Upaniṣads* about *Śrī Devī* [17] – some say that there are 8, some say that there are 17 and further some say there 25. Whatever be the count – there is one called *Śrī Chakra Upaniṣad*. There are no *Veda Upaniṣads* available about *Chakras* pertaining to any other deities. This is another feather on the cap of *Śrī Chakra*.

*****

---

[17] The author of this book is now writing a book detailing the *Upaniṣads* on *Śrī Devī*.

The Form(s) of *Śrī Chakra*

In general, *Śrī Chakra* is considered to be in the form of a drawing in two-dimensional form. But there are some variations in its form.

Yantra: A deity can be worshipped on an idol or picture. This is the physical form of that deity. In a metal sheet, if some lines are drawn according to the prescribed rules that is called **yantra**. This is the subtle form of the deity. In some cult it is a habit to wear this *yantra* as a casket. All the 51 verses of *Kandaranu-būthi*, talk about various *yantras*. Similarly, each of the verse of *Soundaryalaharī* has one *yantra* corresponding to each of it. The *yantras* relating to other deities are also in vogue.

Mantra: The combination of some sounds is called **mantra**. This is still the subtle form of the deity than *yantra*.

An important *yantra* relating to *Śrī Devī* is *Śrī Chakra*. It can be noted that only this *Chakra* has a prefix *Śrī*, which in general means wealth.

Since the *Śrī Chakra* is based on triangles, it is very appropriate that there are currently three main ways to represent this figure – Plane, Pyramidal and Spherical.

Plane: The first and probably the most common is the **plane form.** The inner nine triangles are drawn with straight lines and are contained in circles and squares drawn on a flat plane. *Śrī Chakra* has four upward triangles, five downward triangles and a *bindu* in the center. This *yantra* has Lotus having eight or sixteen petals, three girdles and three border lines. (In some schools it is two border lines. *Śrī Bhāskararāya* says, in his book called *Setu Bandam*, that both the versions are evidenced). In the *Śrī Chakra* in vogue in South India the gates of the border lines are open.

Thus, we get nine halls (*Āvarṇams*). (It is not the practice to treat girdles as *Āvarṇam*). *Āvarṇam* means curtain or fence or compound or fort. The upward triangles are treated as male triangles, belonging to Lord *Śiva* and the five downward triangles are treated as female triangles, belong to *Śakti*. In general, universally, male/ female symbols are upward and downward only.

If the same *Śrī Chakra* is rotated 180 degrees, making the *Śiva* triangles downward then it is called *Śiva Chakra*.

The second is the pyramidal form called *Meru*. Mount Meru is a mythical mountain and hence named because of the mountain shape of the figure. This is basically a 3D version of the plane form. The outline formed by the overlapping triangles is elevated in steps to form a pyramid. If the *Śrī Chakra* is made as a three-dimensional figure (with length, breadth and height), then it is called *Meru*. In fact, the top angle view of the *Meru* is *Śrī Chakra*.

This *Meru/ Śrī Chakra* is of three types, depending on the imagination of the worshippers.

- If it is imagined as unified with 16 *Nityā* [18] *Devīs* it is called *Meru Prastāram*. *Meru Prastāram* is further divided into three types;
  - If in a *Śrī Chakra*, the *Chakras* in threes are called creation, maintenance and destruction (*Śruṣṭi, Stiti* and *Samhāra*) *Chakras*. If the maintenance *Chakras* are little raise than the creation and destruction *Chakra* is further raised, it is one type.
  - The next two lotus are raised than the *Bhūpuras* and again the *Caturdaśara* is further raised, it is second type.

---

[18] 16 *Nityā Devīs* have been discussed in detail in another chapter.

- ○ From *Bhūpuras* till the *Bindu*, each *Chakra* is a little by little raised, it is third type.
- If the *Meru* is unified with 51 *Matrukā* letters (From अ till क्ष) of Samskrutam, it is *Kailāsa Prastāram*.
- When unified with *Vāgdevīs* it is *Bhū Prastāram* – imagining that the *Vāgdevīs* and the *Śrī Chakra* are one and the same. From *Bhūpuras* till the *Bindu*, each *Chakra* is drawn in level.

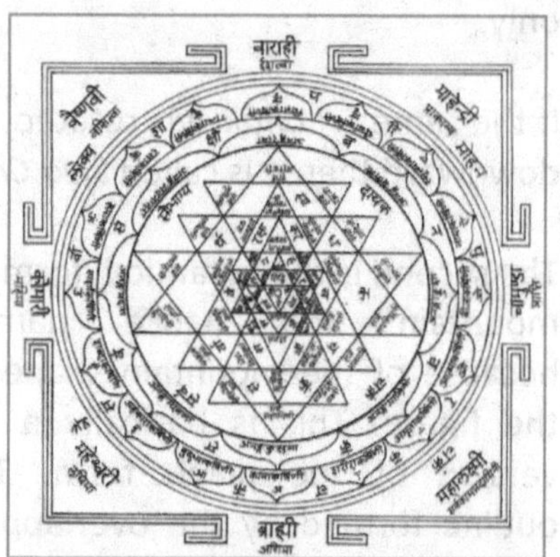

Śrī Chakra With *Matrukā* letters

In some schools a kind of vertically half *Meru* called *Arddha Meru* is also used for worship.

Spherical (*Kūrma*): This is the rarest and the most difficult to reproduce. The figure is drawn or sculpted on a dome shape. The triangles are drawn with curved lines (spherical triangles) making it very difficult to achieve a precise result. *Kūrma* was the second incarnation of Lord Vishnu, the turtle incarnation. This refers to the similarity between this form and the shell of a turtle. It is interesting to note that there seems to be some confusion with the use of these the second and third forms. The pyramidal form is often wrongly referred to as *Kūrma*. This form is the rarest because of the extremely high level of difficulty involved in generating it.

*****

The Power of *Śrī Chakra*

<u>*Tantra of Śrī Chakra*</u>; The *Tantra* of *Śrī Chakra* is called *Śrī Vidyā*. This includes all the essential dimensions of the universe itself. The development of individuality of this whole cosmos, reveals itself, is a practical control.

Hence *tantras*, it connects the structure of the *Śrī Chakra* with the human mode. The six centers in the human body form two groups centering around the cosmic functions. The *Śrī Chakra* activates their reserve centers.

- The *Mūlādhāra* and *Svādhiṣṭāna Chakras* replicate radiation.
- *Maṇipūraka* and *Anāhata Chakras* indicate safety/ security.
- The *Viśuddhi* and *Ajñā Chakras* replicate radiation.

From *Mūlādhāra* till *Viśuddhi*, there are 10 theories – 5 senses (smell, taste, seeing, sound and touching + 5 base elements Ether, Air, Fire, Water and Earth). The centers in the body are also integrated with 3 knots (*grantis*);

1. *Brahma granti* between *Mūlādhāra* and *Svādhiṣṭāna Chakras*.
2. *Viṣṇu granti* between *Maṇipūraka* and *Anāhata Chakras*.
3. *Rudra granti* between *Viśuddhi* and *Ajñā Chakras*.

This has been clearly described by *Śrī Bhāskararāya*, in his *bhāṣyam* for *Śrī Lalitā Sahasranāma*. Still there are different views about the position and names of the *grantis*. Everyone claims that what they have mentioned is the correct one. The details provided by *Śrī Bhāskararāya* is generally accepted by all, since he is *Śrī Vidyā* personified.

Entire *tantra* practice is to awaken the *Kuṇḍalinī* energy sleeping in the Mūlādhāra *Chakra* and take it to the *Sahasrāra Chakra* at the scalp, crossing all the *Chakras* and *grantis*. This is possible only through proper meditation. *Kuṇḍalinī* energy is sleeping like a snake woven around its head for 3.5 anti-clockwise rounds. It has to be woken up and taken through *Suṣumnā Nāḍi*. It has to cross all the 5 other *Chakras* and 3 knots before reaching the highest peak - Bliss, the 1000 petalled *Sahasrāra*

Chakra. This leads to the physical, mental and mental flurry of light (*Brahmānanda*) of the body. This is the culmination of human life.

In our *Sanātana* Hindu religion, what-ever is mentioned in *Vedas* is treated as a recognized one. There is a saying "Is it such a *Veda* saying?" The official note about *Śrī Chakra* can be read in Veda – *Aruṇopaniṣad* chapter 1.27 - verses 114 to 118. The statements in these verses "*AṣṭāChakra Navadvārā*" and "*Devānām Puroyodyā*" describe the *Śrī Chakra* having eight *Chakras*.

Various *Veda* and other books like, *Bāvanopaniṣad, Tripuropaniṣad, Devī Upaniṣad, Soundaryalaharī, Śakti Mahimnā Stotra* by sage *Durvāsa* and so on explain about *Śrī Chakra*, its mathematical construction, its glory, worshipping process/ methods and so many other books. In lot many names, in *Śrī Lalitā Sahasranāma* describe the glory of *Śrī Chakra* and evidence that there is no different between *Śrī Chakra* and *Śrī Lalitā Devī*. To mention some of them;

55	*Sumēru Madhya Śṅrukastā*	सुमेरुमध्यश‍ृङ्गस्ता
230	*Mahā Yāga Kramārātyā*	महायागक्रमाराध्या
245	*Chakra Rāja Nikētaṇā*	चक्रराजनिकेतना
380	*Bindu Maṇḍala Vāsiṇi*	बिन्दुमण्डलवासिनी
775	*Meru Nilayā*	मेरुनिलया
974	*Bindu Tarpaṇa santuṣṭā*	बिन्दुतर्पणसन्तुष्टा
996	*Śrī Chakra Rāja Nilayā*	श्रीचक्रराजनिलया

In another place in *Vedas – Bāvanopaniṣad* of *Atarva Veda*, *Śrī Chakra* has been explained in 37 verses. This attempts to identify and install *Śrī Chakra* with various organs of the human body. This also tries to outline the way in which to consider different parts of *Śrī Chakra* with various organs of human body as explained below. Corresponding names from *Śrī Lalitā Sahasranāma* has also given for comparison.

- *Mūlādhāra* – at the base of the back-bone at the bottom of the body. 99th name in *Śrī Lalitā Sahasranāma – Mūlādhāraikanilayā –* मूलादारैक निलया

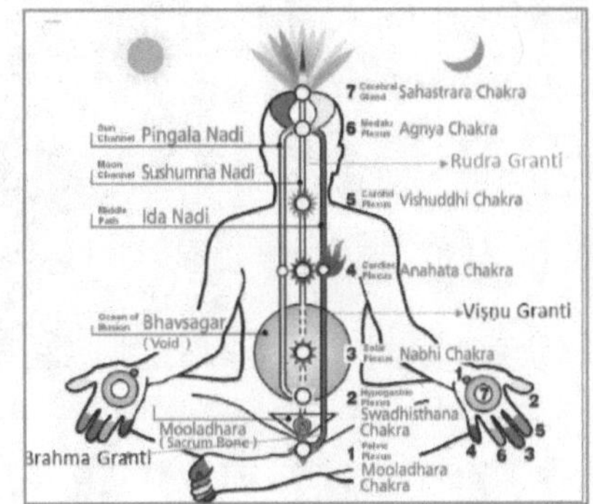

- *Brahma granti* in the middle. 100th name in *Śrī Lalitā Sahasranāma – Brahma-grantivibhedinī –* ब्रह्मग्रन्ति विभेदिनी

- *Svādhiṣṭāna* – at the secret organ. 504th name in *Śrī Lalitā Sahasranāma – Svādhishṭānāmbujagatā –* स्वाधिष्टानाम्बुजगता

- *Maṇipūraka* – at the naval. 101st name in *Śrī Lalitā Sahasranāma – Maṇipūrāntaruditā –* मणिपूरान्तरुदिता

- *Viṣṇu granti* in the middle. 102nd name in *Śrī Lalitā Sahasranāma – Viṣṇugrantivibhedinī –* विष्णुग्रन्ति विभेदिनी

- *Anāhata* – at the heart. 485th name in *Śrī Lalitā Sahasranāma – Anāhatābjanilayā –* अनाहताब्ज निलया

- *Viśuddhi* – at the neck. 475th name in *Śrī Lalitā Sahasranāma – ViśuddhiChakra Nilayā –* विशुद्धिचक्र निलया

- *Rudra granti* in the middle. 104th name in *Śrī Lalitā Sahasranāma – Rudragrantivibhedinī –* रुद्रग्रन्ति विभेदिनी

- *Ajnā* – between the eye-brows. 103rd name in *Śrī Lalitā Sahasranāma – ĀjnāChakrantarālasthā –* आज्ञाचक्रान्त रालस्ता. In *Śrīmad Bhagavad Gīta* also *Śrī Kriṣṇa* conveys that he resides between the eye-brows 'Bruvormadhye'. This emphasizes the significance of *Ājnā Chakram*.

- *Sahasrāra Chakra* – at the scalp. 105th name in *Śrī Lalitā Sahasranāma – Sahasrārāmbujārūḍhā –* सहस्राराम्बुजारूढा.

Bāvanopaniṣad describes this in detail. The word '*Bāvanā*' means imagination or whimsical. The parts of *Śrī Chakra* should be identified with the joints of the human body through imagination and meditated upon. Such a thought should be very serious and strong. This generates a permanent identity of the body with *Śrī Chakra*. Organ by organ and at the end the whole body is regarded as a metaphor of *Śrī Devī* **herself**.

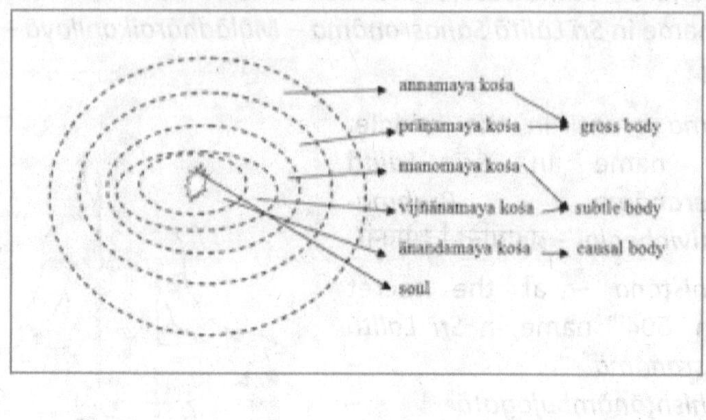

*****

The Geometry of *Śrī Chakra*

Geometrically, the *Śrī Chakra* consists of a number of horizontal and vertical lines, circles, petals and squares. The lines cut across one another and such cutting points are of two kinds – where two lines cut each other it is called a *sandhi* (junction) and where three or more lines cut one another it is called a *marma*. In a *Śrī Chakra* there are 24 *sandhis*, 24 *marmas*, 43 *konas* (corners) and one central *bindu*. All these geometrical figures attract power and concentrate them. It is this concept that makes the *Śrī Chakra* a veritable storehouse of power and energy. This shape and form are something like the pyramids of olden days which still remain an enigma.

In "The Hindu", daily dated 25th November 1984, an article was published about a Russian Scientist who chanced to see a *Śrī Chakra* and tried to describe it by a set of mathematical equations. The following is an extract from that article;

"An algorithm describing *Śrī Yantra*, an involved geometrical diagram created in ancient India has been produced after years of research by Alexi Kulaichev, candidate of Physics and Mathematics, Senior Researcher at the biology faculty of Moscow State University.

The conception of Tantrism on the global dynamics of the Universe is close in some of their details to the Big Bang and Hot Universe Theories.

There is every reason to believe that the *Śrī Yantra* diagram dates from before the first Millennium B.C.E. As the mathematical analysis data obtained by Kulaichev show, *Śrī Yantra* possess several complex properties that pose a problem even for modern science.

His examination of the images' geometrical pattern has revealed that *Śrī Yantra* has a whole array of non-trivial mathematical properties. A strict solution of the geometrical structure requires, according to Kulaichev, the employment of a fairly complex apparatus of modern mathematics (for example – computers to solve numerically a system of non-linear Algebraic equations). To our present way of thinking mathematicians in ancient and medieval India did not dispose of the requisite mathematical and technical facilities, hence the original *Śrī Yantra* appears mysterious in many respects.

Śrī Yantra is a mathematical enigma; Take for example, the Central fragment of the figure – a 14-cornered star formed by the intersection of nine large triangles. The ingenuity of the image is in fact that most of the straight lines forming pass through three, four, five and even six points of interceptions with other lines. To build such a figure and analyze it for an algorithm is an extremely challenging task. It has been accomplished only on a computer, which had to perform more than hundred million operations to do this. Besides, each step-in image building and analysis involved the solution of whole series of related problems, both computation and programmatic.

Śrī Yantra cannot be built by using traditional methods. Only a deep knowledge of such extract sciences as modern higher algebra, numerical analysis and geometry, as well as contemporary mathematical methods can ensure success. I wish to note, however, that the present-day level of scientific and technological knowledge is sometimes insufficient to analyze the structure, for example some stars of *Śrī Yantra* and the number of the possible configurations. Their analysis involves a complex system of algebraic equations and complication calculations, which are beyond the capability of the present generation of computers".

Even after nearly 3 decades most of the above statements are valid. The description and construction of the complete *Śrī Yantra* has its origin from *tantra* literature as given in the commentaries on *Soundaryalaharī*. There are two versions available – One given by *Ādhi Śaṅkara* and the other one given by *Lakshmīdara*. In general, the method given by *Ādhi Śaṅkara* is famous and commonly used by all. Both the methods throw some mathematical errors. However, the error got by *Ādhi Śaṅkara*'s method is very negligible.

*****

Śrī Chakra – Some Facts

A typical *Śrī Chakra* is split into different geometrical figures and the properties of the figures are keenly observed below.

Nine Triangles within a Circle;

Four upward triangles

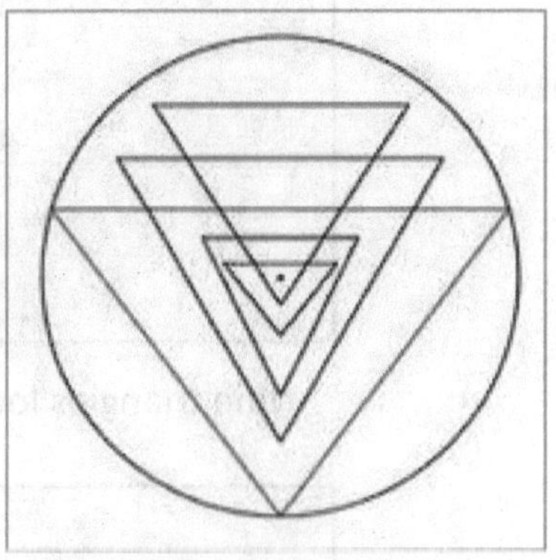

Five downward triangles

Central figure with nine triangles

The intersections of lines of the nine triangles appear as hexagons. The number of black and white areas count to 89 – 43 white and 46 black. The white areas represent energy aspect and the black areas represent the consciousness aspect of reality.

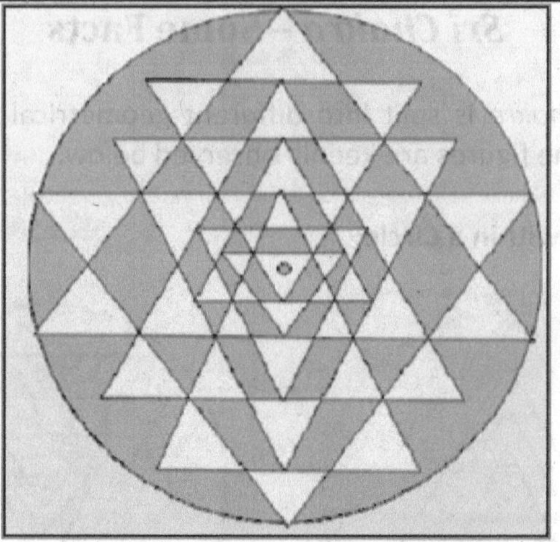

Nine triangles looking like hexagons

The hexagons look like circles

The *Śrī Chakra* is composed of a central figure that is surrounded by two circular rows of petals and then by a rectangular enclosure called the *bhūpura*. If the central figure, comprising of nine overlapping triangles and a *bindu* point, is focused the drawing of *Śrī Chakra* is complete. Four of the triangles pointing upwards, the other five point downwards. In the most popular configuration the two biggest triangles, touch the outer circle on all three points. In some other versions there are either one or two more triangles that touch the outer circle.

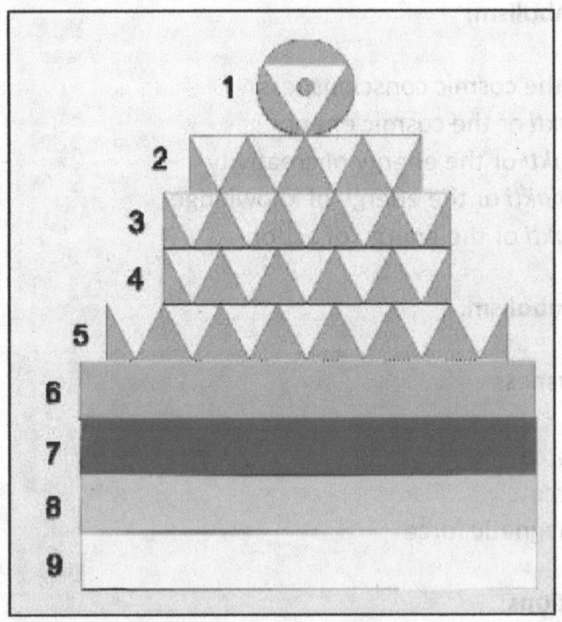

The envelope model of *Śrī Chakra*.

The *Śrī Chakra* is viewed as representing nine consciousness and gravity envelopes as;

1. First *Chakra* – Quantum envelope
2. Second *Chakra* – Particle envelope
3. Third *Chakra* – Atom envelope
4. Fourth *Chakra* – Molecule envelope
5. Fifth *Chakra* – Matter envelope
6. Sixth *Chakra* – Air envelope
7. Seventh *Chakra* – Fire envelope
8. Eighth *Chakra* – Water envelope
9. Ninth *Chakra* – Earth envelope

Symbolisms of *Śrī Chakra*;

Spiritual symbolism;

- *Shiva* or the cosmic consciousness
- *Parā Shakti* or the cosmic energy
- *Icchā Shakti* or the energy of creativity
- *Gnāna Shakti* or the energy of knowledge
- *Kriyā Shakti* or the energy of action

Scientific symbolism;

- Consciousness
- Gravity
- Strong force
- Weak force
- Electromagnetic force

Interconnections;

Triple Intersections

The diagram shows where the triple intersection points are located. These are the points that lock together the triangles. One triangle cannot be moved without moving the others. It can also be noted that the two biggest triangles are touching the outside circle on three points and that the apex of every triangle is connected to the base of another triangle. When looking at the figure it can be observed that there is a **high degree of interconnectedness** between the nine triangles. **This is the main reason why it is so difficult to draw.** This means that every triangle is connected to one or more of the other triangles via common points. Changing the location of one of the triangles usually requires changing the size and position of many other triangles.

Very few *Śrī Chakra* **drawings achieve perfect concurrency;** Mathematically speaking it is not possible. But practically speaking a satisfactory level of precision can be achieved. It is difficult to achieve this when doing the drawing by hand but not impossible. Often the lines are made thicker to hide the errors at the intersections. A good level of accuracy can be achieved with a pencil and ruler and a lot of patience. A better accuracy can be achieved with a drawing program such as Auto-cad or Solid-works. The greatest amount of accuracy will be achieved by using a mathematical program such as Mathematics to compute the figure.

The One and the Many;

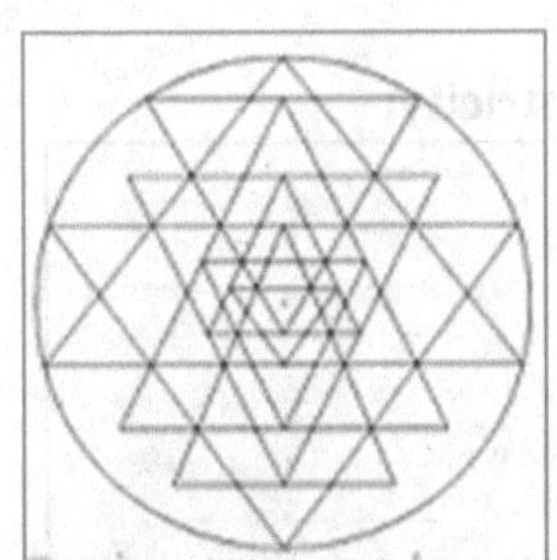

Three different configurations of the *Śrī Chakra.*

It would seem at this point that all one needs to do is to make sure that the lines match precisely at the triple intersections (concurrency) and our job is done – not exactly!

There are different versions of the *Śrī Chakra.* The above shows a few examples. In these examples the differences are obvious. The differences are usually more subtle and require closer examination. Isn't there a **precise and complete** method that would tell us how this famous sacred figure should be drawn? If there is one, we are yet to find it out.

The reason is simple. **The criteria of concurrency** (precise intersections) **are not enough to fully define the *Śrī Chakra*.** Over time people have assumed that being able to produce a figure where the lines meet precisely at the intersections will produce a unique figure. This has led to the current multiplicity of figures available.

To draw a triangle, if the only criteria required is that the figure must have three sides then an infinite number of different triangles with three sides can be drawn. If on the other hand, the triangle is given as having equal sides then there is only one way to draw such a triangle (not taking size into account).

The *Śrī Chakra* is geometry with **five degrees of freedom**, which means that up to five different criteria, can be used to define it. This is why we have to decide on the location of five lines when drawing the figure. Five degrees of freedom is not a lot considering that there is a total of nine triangles. This is because of the high degree of interconnectedness between the triangles. This effectively limits the possibilities and variations that can be achieved.

The Second Key – Concentricity;

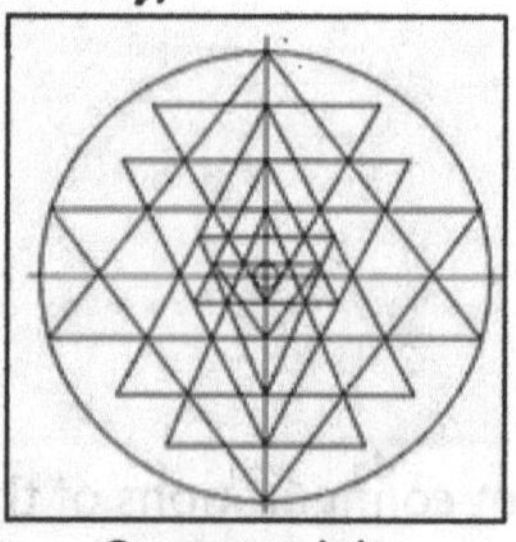

Concentricity

The center of the innermost triangle coincides with the center of the circle. Let us now take a look at the *bindu* point; the small point located in the central triangle. It should be located at the center of the innermost triangle. This can be achieved precisely by placing the *bindu* at the center of the circle that fits inside this triangle. This is known in mathematics as the incenter of a triangle.

To achieve a perfectly centered figure however, the *bindu* should also be located at the center of the outer circle.

The Third Key – Equilateral Inner Triangle;

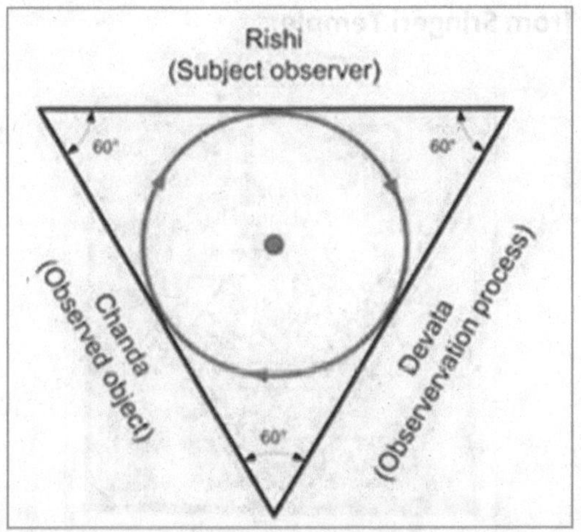

Triangle as the expression of *Rishi*, *Devata* and *Chanda*.

The *Śrī Chakra* symbolizes, among other things the unfoldment of creation. The *bindu* represents the unmanifest, the silent state. The next level in the expression of the Universe is represented by the innermost triangle. This level represents the trinity of *rishi, devata, Chanda*, or the observer, the process of observation and the object being observed. At this point the symmetry of creation is still intact and will be broken when it reaches the next level, which represent the grosser aspects of the relative.

This reflects the unfoldment from unity to trinity as expounded in the Vedic literature. According to the Veda the Universe becomes manifest when unbounded awareness becomes aware of itself. The spark of self-awareness ignites creation. At this point Unity divides into the trinity of *rishi* (the observer), *devata* (process of knowing) and *Chanda* (the object of perception). The same idea is also found in the bible as the principle of the holy trinity.

The central triangle is the central lens of the *Śrī Chakra*. If as some suggest, this pattern is capable of emitting a significant amount of subtle energy, the importance of having a well-balanced and centered figure becomes obvious. For these reasons it is believed that the central triangle should be equilateral in an optimal *Śrī Chakra* configuration. For this to happen the highest down pointing primary triangle must have an angle of 60 degrees.

The *Śrī Chakra* from Śringeri Temple;

Śrī Chakra from Śringeri temple.

Above is a photograph of *Śrī Chakra* encrypted at Śringeri temple. (The photograph is a little smudged. But this is the best possible. Readers are requested to bear). The figure has many of the same characteristics as discussed above. The *bindu* is well centered and more importantly the centermost triangle has an angle very close to 60 degrees. The Sringeri temple in India claims to have the oldest *Śrī Chakra*. This temple is one of the four pillars founded by none other than *Ādhi Śaṅkara* during the first millennium. Assuming that older *Śrī Chakras* are closer to the original configuration – let us see how this *Śrī Chakra* compares to our optimal version. Obviously, it is not possible to be certain that it is the oldest *Śrī Chakra* on Earth but it is certainly older than most of the versions available. *The shape of the petals and the bhūpura are good indicators that it is an old Śrī Chakra configuration.*

<u>The unexplained mystery of the Oregon *Śrī Yantra*;</u>

On August 10, 1990, Bill Miller, a pilot in the Idaho Air National Guard,

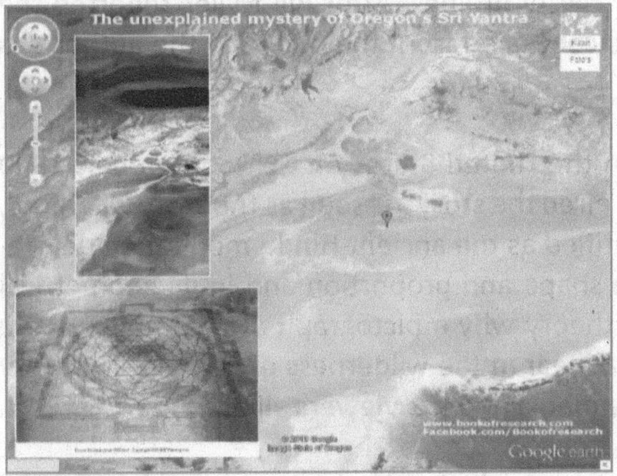

noticed a huge etching on a dried-up lake-bed while flying over it, in Oregon State in the United States. The massive formation was a quarter of a mile in width and was etched 3 inches deep into the surface. In his earlier round about 30 minutes before Miller first noticed the glyph, there had been no trace of this formation. Neither had any of the other pilots of the Idaho National Guard (who regularly train over this corridor), observed any unusual activity or a design-in-process in this area. The etching simply appeared one morning. There was no possibility of any of the other pilots having missed such a prominent formation in process of being made.

The view of *Śrī Yantra* from 9000 feet height – Lieutenant Bill Miller of

the 190th Tactical Recon-naissance Squadron, immediately report-ed the details of what he had spotted to the authorities at the Air National Guard - a 13.3 mile glyph of lines about a quarter of a mile in width and length, on the extremely hard, sunbaked dry bed of a lake in Mickey Basin located southeast of Steens Mountains in the Alvord Desert, 70 miles away from the city of Burns in Oregon.

The Steens Mountain and the Alvord Desert are awe inspiring places. The majestic Steen Mountain rises over a mile from the white plains of the Alvord. The desert is filled with a series of bubbling hot springs and dried-up lakes. The beauty is breathtaking - the ambience mystical!

The formation detected on the morning of August 10, 1990 was oriented precisely in the North-South direction. The glyph had a machine-like precision in its shape and clarity of lines. After Bill Miller reported the observation, the news was concealed from the public by the authorities for thirty days.

The news hit the media in the United States on 12ᵗʰ September, 1990 when Boise TV station first aired the story. As soon as the story was aired, the glyph was quickly identified as the ancient Hindu meditation device- the Sri Yantra- identical in shape and proportion and in its geometrical properties. No one had a theory why a pictograph of a complex Hindu meditation yantra should appear in the wilderness of Oregon. The story caught the attention of the media and the viewers alike.

By September 14ᵗʰ, the story was picked up by the Associated Press, Bend Bulletin and the Oregonian. The Oregonian reported that some architects that had been contacted by the newspaper, had said that the cost of conducting a land survey alone, before such a project could be initiated, would range from 75,000 to 100,000 dollars. The *Śrī Yantra* design has a degree of complexity and a level of symmetry that makes it difficult to recreate its design even on paper, let alone furrow an enormous replication of it on a dry lakebed. There was therefore a good deal of speculation that the glyph was not man-made.

There were other reasons too to support this theory – not the least important of them being the fact that, the shape produced by the lines in this massive Sri Yantra at Oregon, could not be deciphered while standing on the ground. In fact, the shape only made sense when viewed from a height of a few thousand feet above.

The triangles surround and radiate out from a bindu point. The bindu represents the junction point between the physical universe and its un-manifest source. The nine triangles are interlaced in such a way so as to create forty-three smaller triangles symbolic of the entire cosmos.

The *Śrī Yantra* is variedly described as a visual representation of the sound '*Om*' and an expression of the philosophy of '*Advaita*' (one-ness or non-duality). The *Śrī Yantra* is popularly used today in India as a meditation device.

Two UFO Researchers, Don Newman and Alan Decker, visited the site on the morning of 15th September and reported that no trace of tire track markings or foot prints were visible anywhere close to the site even though their own station wagon had now left quarter inch deep marks into the hard crust of the surface along the track from where they had approached the formation.

Dr. James Deardorff, a Research Professor Emeritus at the Atmospheric Science Department of Oregon State University and a colleague of Don Newman and Alan Decker, compiled the details of their investigations and forwarded the story to UFO magazine, a British magazine devoted to the subject of unidentified flying objects (UFOs) and extraterrestrial life. The magazine had an international reputation for quality and authenticity and agreed to publish the story which appeared in Volume 6, # 3 in 1991 under the heading, "A Symbol on the Oregon Desert".

Dr. Deardorff wrote in his investigative story that the government had not been able to give a reasonable explanation to the public as to how a glyph of such a large size had made an undetected appearance on a desolate site, which was constantly patrolled by the Idaho National Air Guard. About forty days after the appearance of the glyph, a group of four people, headed by a Bill Witherspoon, claimed that they had etched out the pictograph, over a period of 10 days, by pulling a garden cultivator like a plow over the lakebed. Mr. Witherspoon said that he had used ropes to ensure that the lines were straight and the angles perfect. Dr. Deardorff countered by saying that the story was concocted and that it was sponsored by the government in its effort to quell the public furor. In all fairness to the government authorities though, it might be added here, that the government was probably acting in what it considers is in the best interest of the general public. The authorities did not want to fuel the belief that the glyph had an unexplained origin.

Bill Witherspoon was interviewed by newspapers to judge the authenticity of his story. Very quickly it became evident that his explanations lacked credibility. The most unconvincing part of his story was his claim that a garden plow, a rope and a blueprint of the formation were enough equipment to furrow out the glyph effortlessly. Bill Witherspoon's electronic interview revealed other incongruities. For one, he had stated in the newspapers that he and his team had carried their tools for three quarters of a mile to the formation site every day for 10 days, however in his video interview he said that he and his team had camped out two miles away from the site.

Bill Witherspoon's team only managed to gouge out a ½ inch deep line with great exertion when they were asked to demonstrate how they had gouged out 13.3 miles of lines, 3 inches deep and 10 inches wide. The line lacked neatness, and, the displaced soil fell unevenly on the two sides of the carved line. No one believed anymore that the original glyph could have been created by using crude tools such as garden plows.

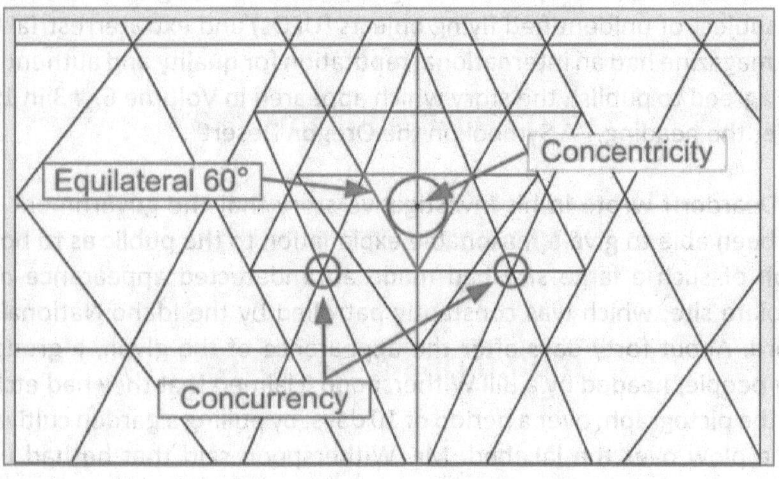

Three Characteristics of location of the *Śrī Yantra*

*****

Śrī Chakra – **Mathematical Construction**

Drawing a *Śrī Chakra* becomes a lot more complex mainly because the triangles are interconnected. If one triangle is moved, all the others are also having to be moved, so that they will intersect properly. With enough time or with the aid of computers and mathematics, it is possible to draw a figure where the intersections match perfectly. But it turns out that this is not enough to fully define the figure. This criterion in itself is not enough to produce a unique figure. This is the reason there are so many different versions of the *Śrī Chakra* in circulation.

The central figure is composed of nine interlocking triangles. Every triangle is connected to the others by common points and that is the reason it is so difficult to draw accurately. Changing the size or position of one triangle often require changing the position of many other triangles.

Drawing *Śrī Chakra* is not as easy as it looks. Given the fact that this is one of the oldest and most recognizable sacred geometry one would assume that a method for drawing this famous figure precisely would be easy to find. The method of starting from the border lines and ending with *Bindu* is called destructive (*laya*[19]) method. On the other hand, starting from the *Bindu* and ending with border lines is called creative method. Mostly only the *laya* method is in practice.

The great commentator on *Soundaryalaharī*, *Śrī Lakshmīdara* describes two methods of drawing the *Śrī Chakra*, one starting from the point of view of creation with the *Bindu* as the originating point and the other from the point of view of dissolution of the Universe. The latter starts from the outer *Bhūpura* and ends at the central *Bindu*. This is the method by which the *Āvaraṇa pooja* or worship is generally performed.

The traditional method described by *Śrī* Lakśmīdara and widely accepted by the scholars, requires the diameter of a circle to be divided into 48 parts and marking off consequently 6, 6, 5, 3, 4, 3, 3, 6, 6 and 6 parts, making up the full diameter. The procedure further goes on to construct the five triangles with apexes downwards and four triangles with apexes

---

[19] The initial vacum is called '*laya*' and the final one is called '*samādhi*'.

upwards. These proportions are accurate enough for small sizes of the *Śrī Chakra*.

Analyzing the figure trigonometrically by "solution of triangles", the minimum data for the construction is taken in the beginning and additional locations are derived as the construction proceeds. The proportions are also adjusted to result in higher accuracy of the *marmas*. The traditional proportions of 6, 6, 5, 3, 4, 3, 3, 6, 6 and 6 give an error of 1.1 % and the proportions suggested further reduces the error to 0.1 %, which is considered as an improvement. It may be possible to improve further the accuracy by refining the data further.

This author has drawn the *Śrī Chakra* using Auto-cad and the method of construction with step-by-step drawings has been explained in his other book. Fearing the size and focus of this book, further details are not discussed here.

Thus far, we tried to understand something about and around *Śrī Chakra* and its nuances. Let us delve something on the *upāsana* front.

*****

Mudras

A (मुद्रा), *mudrā*, 'seal', 'mark', or 'gesture' is a symbolic or ritual gesture or pose in Hinduism, Jainism and Buddhism. The origin of the word *mudra* (signet) can be explained in two different ways. One explanation is *mudam rāti* – i.e. giving happiness. This happiness is for both – one who shows the signet and to whom it is shown.

The second explanation is *Modanāt, Drāvanāt* – i.e. it is called as *mudra* since it makes the person to whom it is shown as happy and it drives away the sins of the person who shows it. The meaning of the word *Drāvanāt* has been given as that it drives away the universe from the mind of the worshipper – i.e. the mind set of dualities.

While some mudras involve the entire body, most are performed with the hands and fingers. A hand sign is an important communication in the body language, expressing our joy without any desire. As well as being spiritual gestures employed in the iconography and spiritual practice, *mudras* have meaning in many forms of Sri Vidya Upasana, Indian dance and yoga. The range of *mudras* used in each field (and religion) differs, but with some overlap. In addition, many of the Buddhist *mudras* are used outside South Asia and have developed different local forms elsewhere.

In *hatha yoga*, *mudras* are used in conjunction with *pranayama* (yogic breathing exercises), generally while in a seated posture, to stimulate different parts of the body involved with breathing and to affect the flow of *pranan*. It is also associated with *bindu, bodhicitta, Amruta* and consciousness in the body. Unlike older tantric *mudras, hatha yogic mudras* are generally internal contractions, involving the pelvic floor, diaphragm, throat, eyes, tongue, anus, genitals, abdomen and other parts of the body. Examples of this diversity of *mudras* are *Moola Bandha, Mahamudra, Viparita Karani* and *Khecarī mudrā*. These expanded in number from three in the *Amrita siddhi*, to 25 in the *Gheranda Samhita*, with a classical set of ten arising in the *Hatha Yoga Pradipika*.

Mudra is used in the iconography of Hindu and Buddhist art of the Indian subcontinent and described in the scriptures, such as the *Nātyaśāstra*, which lists 24 *asaṁyuta* (separated, meaning "one-hand") and 13 *saṁyuta* (joined, meaning "two-hands") *mudras*. *Mudra* positions are usually formed by both the hand and the fingers. Along with *āsanas* (seated postures), they are employed statically in meditation and dynamically in the *Nāṭya*.

Hindu and Buddhist iconography share some *mudras*. In some regions, for example in Laos and Thailand, these are distinct but share related iconographic conventions.

The word mudrā has Sanskrit roots. According to scholar Sir Monier-Williams it means 'seal' or "any other instrument used for sealing". He has also defined it as, "a general noun for certain positions or intertwining of the fingers commonly practiced in devotion or religious worship and held to be symbolical".

In Laos and Thailand, a Buddha image can have one of several common *mudras*, combined with different *asanas*. The main *mudras* used to represent specific moments in the life of the Buddha and are shorthand depictions of these.

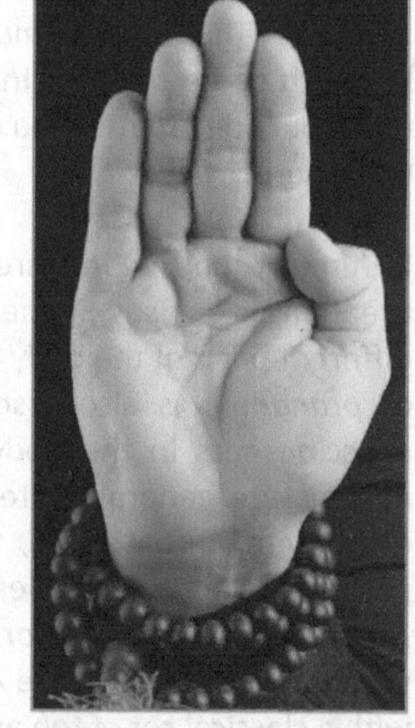

Abhaya mudrā or Leela attitude – The Abhaya mudra (gesture of fearlessness) represents protection, peace, benevolence and the dispelling of fear. It is usually made while standing with the right arm bent and raised to shoulder height, the palm facing forward, the fingers closed, pointing upright and the left hand resting by the side. Generally, this mudra can be seen in all temples and on the idols of all deities. In Thailand and Laos, this mudra is associated with the Walking Buddha, sometimes also shown having both hands making a double Abhaya mudrā that is uniform.

This mudrā was probably used before the onset of Buddhism as a symbol of good intentions proposing friendship when approaching strangers. In Gandharan art, it is seen when showing the action of preaching. It was also used in China during the Wei and Sui eras of the 4th and 7th centuries.

This gesture was used by the Buddha when attacked by an elephant, subduing it as shown in several frescoes and scripts. In Mahayana Buddhism, the deities are often portrayed as pairing the *Abhaya mudrā* with another mudrā using the other hand.

Bhūmisparśa mudrā – *Maravijaya* attitude – The *bhūmisparśa* ("earth witness") *mudrā* of Gautama Buddha is one of the most common iconic images of Buddhism. Other names include "Buddha calling the earth to witness" and "earth-touching". It depicts the story from Buddhist legend of the moment when Buddha attained complete enlightenment, with Buddha sitting in meditation with his left hand, palm upright, in his lap, and his right hand touching the earth. In the legend, Buddha was challenged by the evil one, Mara, who argue for a witness to attest his right to achieve it. In response to Mara, Buddha touched the ground, and Phra Mae Thorani, the earth goddess, appeared to be the witnesses for the Buddha's enlightenment.

In East Asia, this mudra (also called the Maravijaya attitude) may show Buddha's fingers not reaching as far as the ground, as is usual in Burmese or Indian depictions.

Bodhyangi mudrā – The Bodhyangi mudrā, the "mudrā of the six elements," or the "fist of wisdom," is a gesture entailing the left-hand index finger being grasped with the right hand. It is commonly seen on statues of the *Vairocana Buddha*.

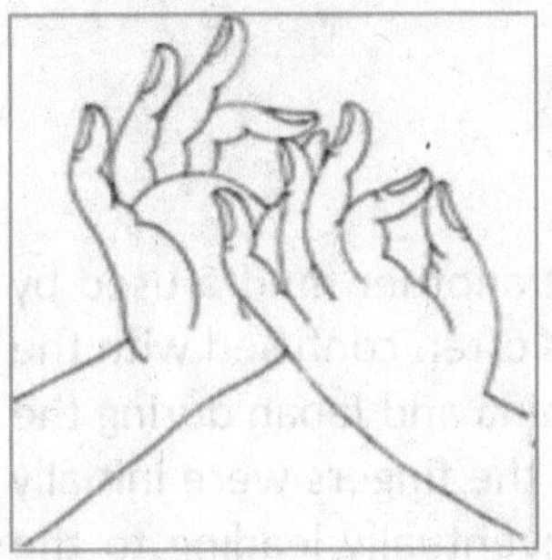

Dharmachakra Pravartana mudrā – The Buddha preached his first sermon after his Enlightenment in Deer Park in Sarnath. The Dharmachakra Pravartana or "turning of the wheel" *mudrā* represents that moment. In general, only Gautama Buddha is shown making this mudrā except Maitreya as the dispenser of the Law. Dharmachakra mudrā is two hands close together in front of the chest in vitarka with the right palm forward and the left palm upwards, sometimes facing the chest. There are several variants such as in the Ajanta Caves frescoes, where the two hands are separated and the fingers do not touch. In the Indo-Greek style of Gandhara, the clenched fist of the right hand seemingly overlies the fingers joined to the thumb on the left hand.

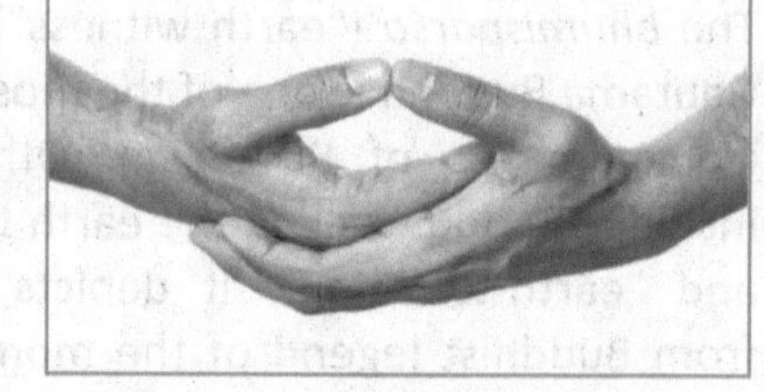

Dhyāna mudrā – Meditation attitude – The *dhyāna mudrā* ("meditation mudra") is the gesture of meditation, of the concentration of the Good Law and the sangha. The two hands are placed on the lap, with the right hand resting on the left and the fingers fully extended. The four fingers rest on each other and the thumbs face diagonally upward towards each other, with the palms facing upwards. Together, the hands and fingers form the shape of a triangle, which is symbolic of the spiritual fire or the Three Jewels. This mudrā is used in representations of Gautama Buddha and Amitābha. The dhyāna mudrā is sometimes used in representations of Bhaiṣajyaguru as the "Medicine Buddha", with a medicine bowl placed on the hands. It originated in India, most likely in Gandhāra and then in China during the Northern Wei dynasty.

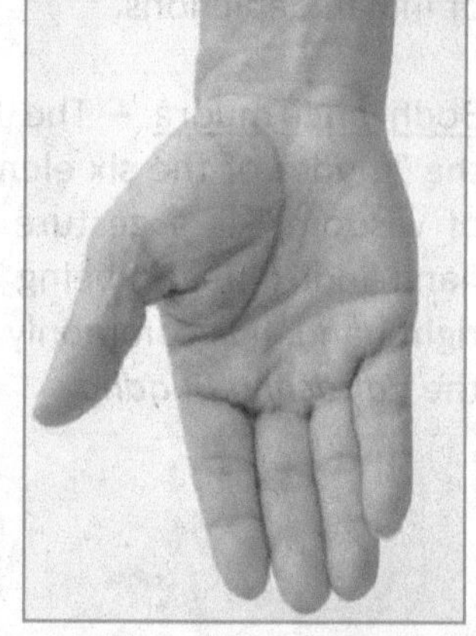

Varada mudrā – The *Varadamudrā* ("generosity gesture") signifies offering, welcome, charity, giving, compassion and sincerity. It is nearly always shown with the left hand by a revered figure devoted to human salvation from greed, anger and delusion. It can be made with the arm bent and the palm turned slightly upward, or, in when the arm faces downwards, the palm presented with the fingers upright or slightly bent. The Varada mudrā is rarely seen without another mudrā used by the right hand, typically the Abhaya mudrā. It is often confused with the Vitarka mudrā, which it closely resembles. In China and Japan during the Northern Wei and Asuka periods, respectively, the fingers were initially stiff and then gradually loosened over time, eventually leading to the Tang dynasty standard where the fingers are naturally curved.

In India, Varada mudra is used by both seated and standing figures, of Buddha, Bodhisattvas and other figures, and in Hindu art is especially associated with Vishnu. It was used in images of Avalokiteśvara from Gupta art (4th and 5th centuries) onwards. The Varada mudrā is widely used in statues of Southeast Asia.

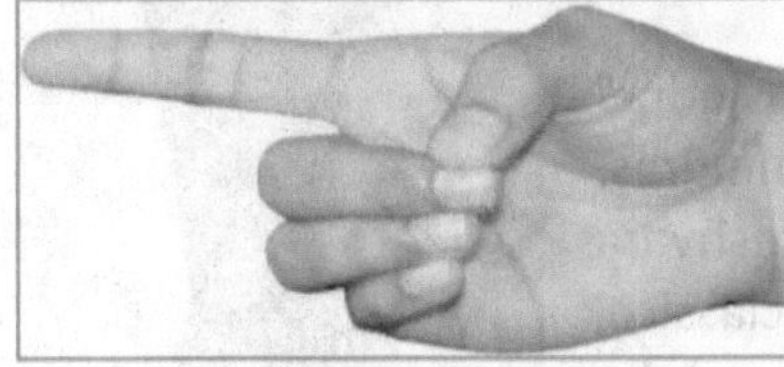

Vajra mudrā – The Vajra mudrā ("thunderbolt gesture") is the gesture of knowledge.

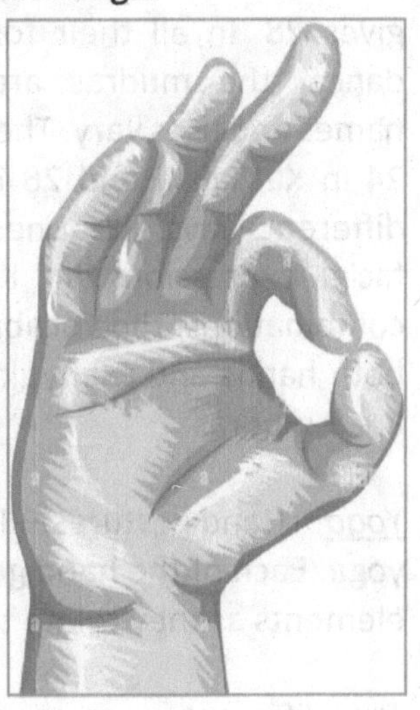

Vitarka mudrā – The Vitarka mudrā ("mudra of discussion") is the gesture of discussion and transmission of Buddhist teaching. It is formed by joining the tips of the thumb and the index together, and keeping the other fingers straight, similar to the Abhaya and Varada mudrās but with the thumbs touching the index fingers. This mudrā has many variants in Mahayana Buddhism. In Tibetan Buddhism, it is a ritual gesture of Tārās and bodhisattvas, with some variations by the deities in Yab-Yum. The Vitarka mudrā is also known as Vyākhyāna mudrā ("mudra of explanation"). This is also called as chin-mudra.

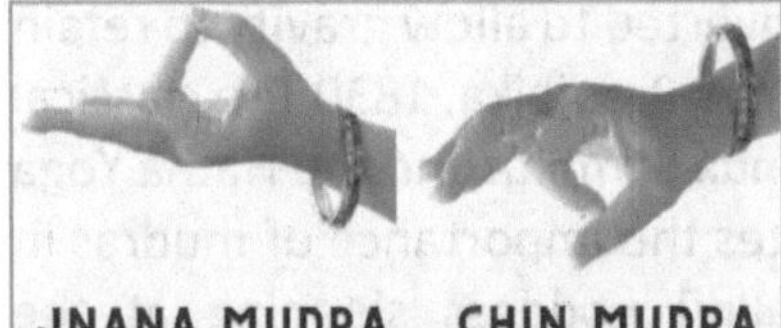

Jñāna mudrā – Jnana yoga – The Jñāna mudrā ("mudra of wisdom") is formed by touching the tips of the thumb and the index together to form a circle, with the hand-held palm inward towards Jnana the heart. The mudrā represents spiritual enlightenment in Indian-origin religions. Sometimes sadhus chose to be buried alive in this samadhi position. A 2700-year-old skeleton arranged in this position was found at Balathal in Rajasthan, suggesting that practices resembling yoga may have existed at that time.

Karaṇa mudrā – The karaṇa mudrā is the mudrā which expels demons and removes obstacles such as sickness or negative thoughts. It is made by raising the index and the little finger while folding the other fingers. It is nearly the same as the Western "sign of the horns", however, in the Karana mudrā the thumb does not hold down the middle and ring fingers. This mudrā is also known as tarjanī mudrā.

In Indian classical dance the term "Hasta Mudra" is used. The Natya Shastra describes 24 mudras, while the Abhinaya Darpana of Nandikeshvara gives 28. In all their forms of Indian classical dance, the mudras are similar, though the names and uses vary. There are 28 (or 32) root mudras in Bharatanatyam, 24 in Kathakali and 28 in Odissi. These root mudras are combined in different ways, like one hand, two hands, arm movements, body and facial expressions. In Kathakali, which has the greatest number of combinations, the vocabulary adds up to C.E. 900. Sanyukta mudras use both hands and asanyukta mudras use one hand. In Thai dances, there are 9 mudras.

Yoga – Hand gestures – There are numerous hand gesture mudras in yoga. Each of the hand gestures is based on the concept of the five elements as they relate to one's fingers.

The different yoga mudras involve different parts of the body and correspondingly diverse procedures, generally to retain the vital energy of prana. In Viparita Karani, the body is inverted to allow gravity to retain the bindu. Illustrated manuscript of the Joga Pradipika, 1830 The classical sources for the yogic seals are the Gheranda Samhita and the Hatha Yoga Pradipika. The Hatha Yoga Pradipika states the importance of mudras in yoga practice: "Therefore the [Kundalini] goddess sleeping at the entrance of Brahma's door [at the base of the spine] should be constantly aroused with all effort, by performing mudra thoroughly." In the 20th and 21st centuries, the yoga teacher Satyananda Saraswati, founder of the Bihar School of Yoga, continued to emphasize the importance of mudras in his instructional text Asana, Pranayama, Mudrā, Bandha.

Hatha yoga – The yoga mudras are diverse in the parts of the body involved, the procedures required, and the supposed effects, as in Moola Bandha, Mahamudra, Viparita Karani and Khecarī mudrā.

Moola Bandha – Mode of action of mudras, serving to trap energy-fluids (breath, prana, bindu, Amruta) and thus help to unblock the central sushumna Nadi (channel). Mula Bandha, the Root Lock, consists of pressing one heel into the anus, generally in a cross-legged seated asana, and contracting the perineum, forcing the prana to enter the central sushumna channel.

Mahamudra – (Hatha Yoga) Mahamudra, the Great Seal, similarly has one heel pressed into the perineum; the chin is pressed down to the chest in Jalandhara Bandha, the Throat Lock, and the breath is held with the body's upper and lower openings both sealed, again to force the prana into the sushumna channel.

Viparita Karani, the Inverter, is a posture with the head down and the feet up, using gravity to retain the prana. Gradually the time spent in the posture is increased until it can be held for "three hours". The practice is claimed by the Dattatreya yoga shastra to destroy all diseases and to banish grey hair and wrinkles.

Khecarī mudrā – the Khechari Seal, consists of turning back the tongue "into the hollow of the skull", sealing in the bindu fluid so that it stops dripping down from the head and being lost, even when the yogi "embraces a passionate woman". To make the tongue long and flexible enough to be folded back in this way, the Khechari vidya exhorts the yogi to make a cut a hair's breadth deep in the frenulum of the tongue once a week. Six months of this treatment destroys the frenulum, leaving the tongue able to fold back; then the yogi is advised to practice stretching the tongue out, holding it with a cloth, to lengthen it, and to learn to touch each ear in turn, and the base of the chin. After six years of practice, which cannot be hurried, the tongue is said to become able to close the top end of the sushumna channel.

The Mudras play an important role in Sri Vidya, especially in Navavarna Pujas. There are 'n' number of Mudras, but 16 of them are treated as main and 10 out of them more so are treated as more important. They are called as Dasha Maha Mudras. In the practice of _Sri Vidya Sadhana_, the significance of the ten mudras is deeply profound. Ten signets, in a combined form, have been mentioned in 977th name of Sri Lalitā Sahasranāma, _Dashamudrāsamārādhya_. It is easy to know these signets by seeing them in person when somebody shows it. These are shown in *Navāvarṇa* worship.

These captures the essence of worshipping the divine through these ten sacred hand gestures, known as *mudras*. These gestures are not merely physical postures. They are a rich form of symbolic sign language intricately designed to communicate with the Goddess herself. Each mudra is imbued with powerful *bījākṣaras* (seed syllables), which activate various dimensions of the spiritual journey. Through these *mudras*, practitioners engage with the divine, channeling their inner energies and intentions, thus deepening their spiritual connection and enhancing their transformation.

These mudras are not merely symbolic but esoteric gestures embodying divine forces. When a Sādhaka performs these gestures, they enact a sacred dialogue with the Goddess. Each mudra taps into specific energies.

The Dasha mudras are deeply personal and should not be displayed publicly, as seen by lay men. It can be reminded that more than once it has been stressed that *Śrī Vidyā* worship has to be kept secret. These signets can be shown only during worship times. They are sacred gestures exchanged between the sadhaka and the Goddess as a divine conversation. When performing these mudras, the sādhaka is asking for permission to interact with the Goddess, and only when she grants permission through the final *Sarva-trikhaṇḍe Mudrā* can the full communion take place. Further those who aim at salvation these signets should be shown through mental desire and others can show them through hands. Let us try to comprehend one by one;

1. *Sarva-saṃkṣobhiṇī Mudrā*

This mudra invokes the power to agitate and transform. This Indicates the creation of the entire universe by the illusion of the static energy imagined from the pure conscious energy.

- The Bījākṣara of this Mudra is *drāṁ*. The energy of *drāṁ* stirs up the world of perception, awakening the mind to higher realities.

- This pertains to first Avaranam – Trilokya Mohana chakram.
- Chakra beeja mantra – *Am Aam Souḥ*
- Relevant yoginis – *Prakata Yoginis*
- Presiding Deity – Tripura Sundari

2. *Sarva-vidrāviṇī Mudrā*

This mudra dispersion, the ability to dissolve illusions and attachments, clearing the path to higher spiritual knowledge. Indicates the status of the universe (the status enjoyed by the five knowledge organs).

- The Bījākṣara of this Mudra is *drīṁ*.
- This pertains to Tvitheeya (second) avaranam – *Sarvasa Paripooraka chakram*.
- Chakra beeja mantra – *Aim Klim Souḥ*
- Relevant yoginis – *Gupta Yoginis*
- Presiding Deity – Tripuresi

3. *Sarvā-karṣiṇī Mudrā*

This mudra draws desired energies or blessings, pulling them towards the practitioner. Indicates the state of the mind with the knowledge (after the above enjoyment) in a subtle form (i.e. the remembering of the enjoyments).

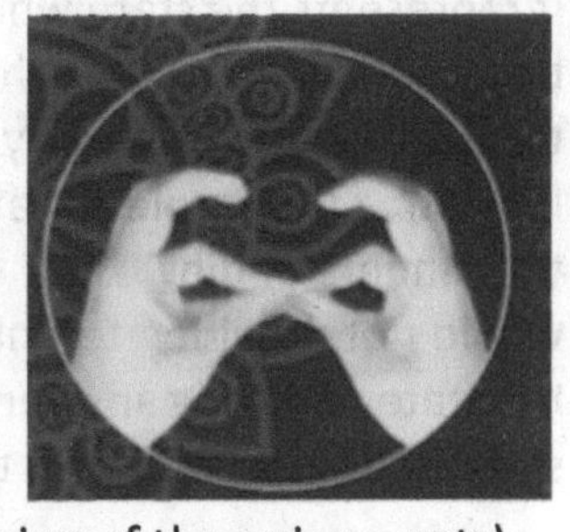

- The *Bījākṣara* of this Mudra is *Klīṁ*.
- This pertains to Tritiya (third) avaranam – Sarva *samkshobhana chakram*.
- Chakra beeja mantra – *Hreem Klim Souḥ*
- Relevant yoginis – *Guptatara Yoginis*
- Presiding Deity – Tripura Sundari

4. *Sarva-vaśaṃkarī Mudrā*

Blūṁ represents control. This mudra exerts influence over the surrounding world, helping to align external circumstances with divine will. Indicates the matters that would be enjoyed by mind and the organs as well. The happiness and the sorrows of the enjoyer – i.e. the bliss status of the enjoyer (including the sorrows).

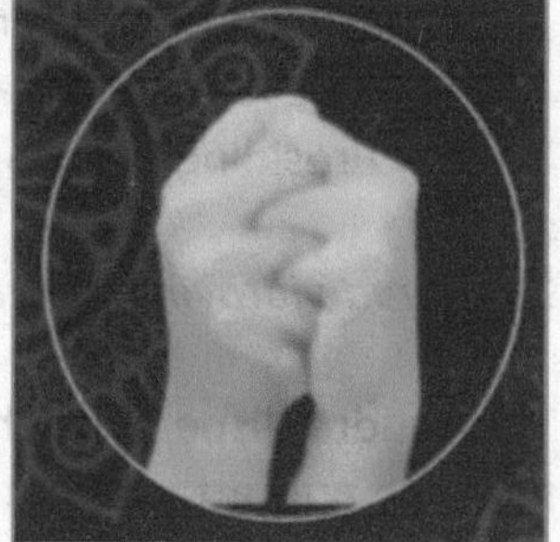

- The Bījākṣara of this Mudra is *Blūṁ*.
- This pertains to Thureeya (fourth) avaranam – Sarva *saubhagya dayaka chakram*.
- Chakra beeja mantra – *Haim Hakleem Hasouḥ*
- Relevant yoginis – *Sampradaya Yoginis*
- Presiding Deity – Tripura Vasini

5. *Sarvon-mādinī Mudrā*

It represents the state where the practitioner becomes one with the cosmic dance, transcending ordinary consciousness. Indicating the careless state of the mind after the understanding that the worldly affairs

would not provide eternal happiness, understand the flaws in them and the state of having an aversion to the experience of the universe – i.e. the state of determination in the mind.

- The Bījākṣara of this Mudra is *souḥ*. *Souḥ* symbolises the maddening joy and divine intoxication.
- This pertains to Panchama (fifth) avaranam – Sarvartha *sadhaka chakram*.
- Chakra beeja mantra – *Hasaim Haskleem Hasouḥ*
- Relevant yoginis – *Kulotteerna Yoginis*
- Presiding Deity – Tripurashree

The first five *bījākṣaras* (*drāṁ, drīṁ, klīṁ, blūṁ, souḥ*) correspond to the five arrows of Manmatha, the god of love, symbolising sensory pleasures.

These *bījākṣaras* also represent the five senses: sound (*śabda*), touch (*sparśa*), sight (*rūpa*), taste (*rasa*) and smell (*gandha*), reflecting the individual's interaction with the world.

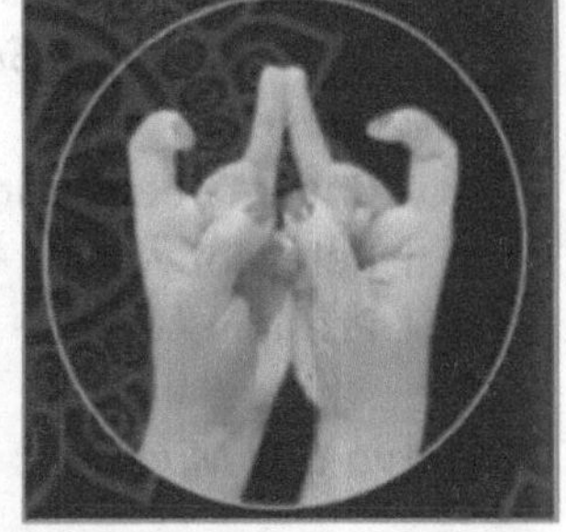

6. *Sarva-mahānkuśa Mudrā*

This represents the cutting of ties with the six enemies of the mind: lust, anger, greed, delusion, pride, and jealousy. Even after having the determination, because of its previous experience the mind may turn out to the outward enjoyments. This indicates the focusing of the mind, at that time and making it looking inwardly. i.e. Meditating upon the self–realisation.

- The Bījākṣara of this Mudra is *krom*. Krom is the embodiment of anger and control. Just as the ankuśa (elephant goad, bullhook) guides an elephant, this mudra also guides the sadhaka away from negative forces and towards spiritual focus. It signifies mastery over internal enemies like lust, greed, and attachment.
- This pertains to *Shashta* (sixth) avaranam – Sarva *Rakshakara chakram*.
- Chakra beeja mantra – *Hreem kleem bleam*
- Relevant yoginis – *Nigarbha Yoginis*
- Presiding Deity – Tripuramalini

7. *Sarva-khecarī Mudrā*

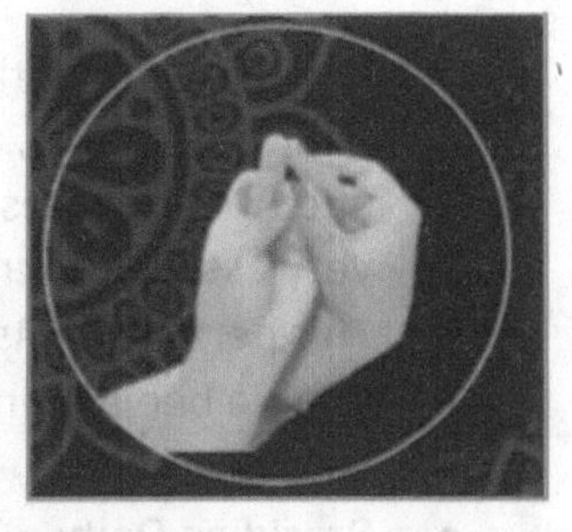

This mudra allows the practitioner to fly through space, symbolically freeing themselves from earthly bondage. Khecarī means 'Skywalker', and the *bījākṣara* signifies transcendence through the fire of knowledge. Through the fire of phrem, the sādhaka transcends all limitations, experiencing unity with the cosmic void. Indicates the expansion of the mind that would involve in the broad supreme being. i.e. it can also be construed as remembering the great statements.

- The Bījākṣara of this Mudra is *hskhphreṁ. Hskhphreṁ* indicates flight beyond earthly limitations. The syllable kha means 'space', while Ha and Sa symbolise Śiva and Śakti.
- This pertains to *Saptama* (seventh) avaranam – Sarva *Roga Hara chakram.*
- Chakra beeja mantra – *Hrīm Śrīm Souḥ*
- Relevant yoginis – *Rahasya Yoginis*
- Presiding Deity – *Tripura Siddhā*

8. *Sarva-bīja Mudrā*

The mudra Hsauṁ represents the eternal union of Shiva and Shakti, symbolising the balance between creation and existence. This sacred union gives rise to everything: the manifested world and the unmanifested realm, with pure consciousness intertwined with the dynamic energy flowing through the universe. By performing this mudra, one invokes the blessings of the Goddess, inviting her divine wisdom and knowledge to flow into the sadhaka. It acts as a bridge, connecting the practitioner to profound insights and the timeless truths of existence. The self–form is the only cause of the universe. Hence it indicates that only the soul is the dwelling place and the brightness for the entire universe. i.e. it indicates *nitityāsana*.

- The Bījākṣara of this Mudra is *hsouṁ*. Hsauṁ invokes the union of Śiva and Śakti, where Ha represents Śiva, Sa represents Śakti, and Auṁ denotes their cosmic union. This mudra taps into the very essence of creation.
- This pertains to *Ashtama* (Eigth) avaranam – Sarva *Sidhi chakram.*
- Chakra beeja mantra – *Hsraim Hsklrīm Hsrouḥ*
- Relevant yoginis – *Athi Rahasya Yoginis*
- Presiding Deity – *Tripurāmbā*

9. *Sarva-yonī Mudrā*

Simply called as *Yoni mudra* itself. This signifies the divine womb, the source of all creation. Through this mudra, the practitioner connects with the body's seven energy centers (chakras). Indicates the union of the soul with the *brahmam*. i.e. the state of *savikalpa samādhi* (the initial temporary state of the spiritual state of consciousness).

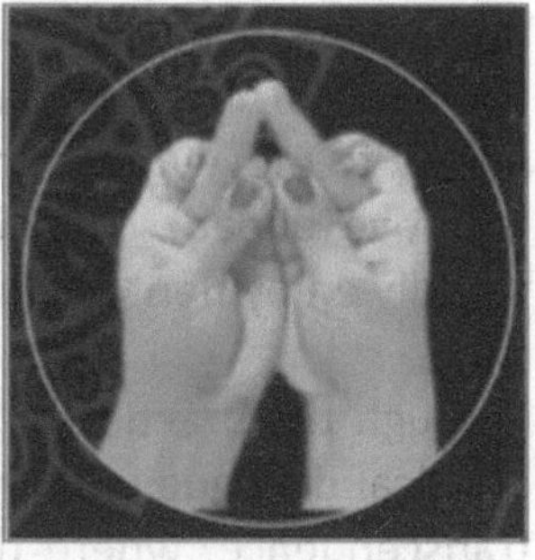

- The Bījākṣara of this Mudra is *Aiṁ*. *Aiṁ* represents creation and causality.
- This pertains to *Navama* (Nineth) avaranam – Sarvānandamaya *chakram*.
- Chakra beeja mantra – *Pancadaśī/ Ṣodaśī Moola Mantra*
- Relevant yoginis – *Parā Parādhi Rahasya Yoginis*
- Presiding Deity – *Lalitā Mahā Tripura Sundari*

10. *Sarva-trikhaṇḍe Mudrā*

This mudra is the culmination of the entire process. This is when the Goddess bestows her consent, allowing you to engage in communion with Her. This indicates the salvation state of the soul.

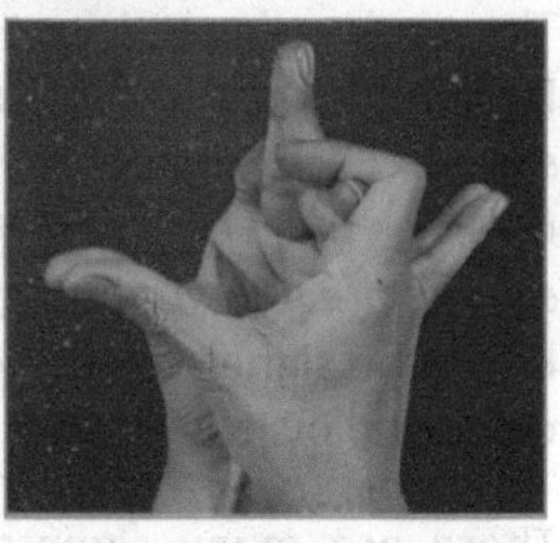

These energies manifest in the forms of:

1. Sarasvatī (Icchā) – represents pure knowledge.
2. Lakṣmī (Jñāna) – represents wisdom and discernment.
3. Kālī (Kriyā) – represents the power of action and transformation.

Out of these, while establishing *Śrī Devī* during *Navāvarṇa* worship in *yantra* (either in *Śrīchakra* or *Meru*) the signet called *Trikhandā* is shown. The worshippers of *Shoḍasee*, while performing worship to *Bindu* after the ninth *Āvarṇa* show this signet. This can be taken as the combined form of all the signets. It can be noted that *Śrī Devī* is called as *Trikhaṇḍeshee* in the 983rd name of Sri Lalita Sahasranama.

By showing these signets the presiding deities in the concerned *Āvaranas*, the head of *chakras*, *Siddhis* and the *mudra Devīs* get satisfied. They permit to move ahead to next *Āvaranas*. (i.e. they provide the mind set to move ahead). The Mudra deities are capable of bestowing both worldly enjoyment and liberation.

Through the practice of these sacred *mudrās*, the sadhaka steps into a mystical dialogue with the Divine Mother. Each gesture is a gateway to transcendence, where the material world intertwines with the divine. The mudras are more than physical gestures; they are potent vibrations harmonising the practitioner's inner self with the universal rhythm. By aligning body, mind, and spirit with the Goddess, the sadhaka invites a deep, transformative connection, where boundaries between the self and the divine dissolve, revealing the infinite wisdom and grace in the heart of existence. The journey is one of surrender, where each mudra unlocks a new layer of understanding, gently guiding the soul toward liberation and oneness with the Goddess.

The mudra, signet, is one of the five important parts of *Śrīvidya* worship. By combining the fingers and showing it in a particular form is called signet. Each signet, cryptically, indicates a message or an emotion. We all know that such signets are shown during dancing. Those who know the signet can understand the message conveyed by it.

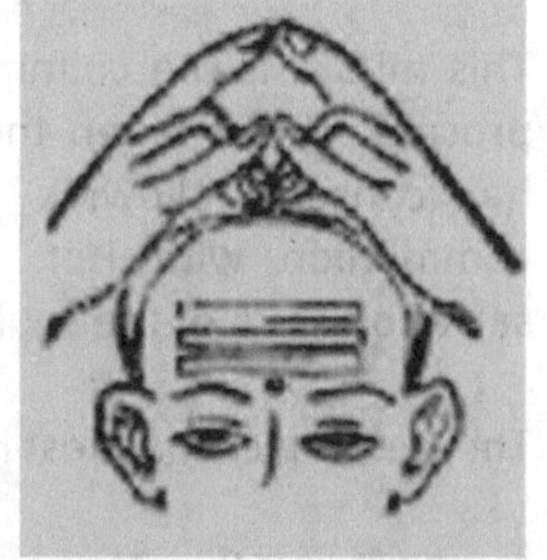

There are many signets in worshipping *Śrī Vidyā*. It is the practice to show the deer sign when chanting the *guru patukā* (chappals of teacher) *mantras* and immediately followed by the signs of *sumukha* (good face), *suvruddha* (good development),

mudgara and *chaturasra* (fourth) and with the *yoni* sign to pray the teacher and *Gaṇapati* respectively in the left and right shoulders.

There are signs to be shown in *Navāvarṇa* worship during *Āvāhanam*, *Nyāsa*, *Pātrasādanam* and *Nivedanam*. The 122nd name *Shāmbhavee*, in Sri Lalita Sahasraṇama, is not accounted here since its fundamental meaning is consort of *Shambu*. Further *Shāmbhavee* signet has been mentioned in *yoga sāstra* and not in Sri Vidya worship. There are multiple names in Sri Lalita *sahasranāma* with names of signets.

In 979th name *Gnānamudra* has been mentioned. This is also called as <u>chinmudra</u>. It is to show the round symbol by joining the thumb and the forefinger of the right hand. *Paramashiva*, in the form of *Dakshiṇāmoorthi* by keeping silent teaches the unison of *Brahmam*—soul to *Sanakā* and other sages, through this signet. (*Śrī Ādi*

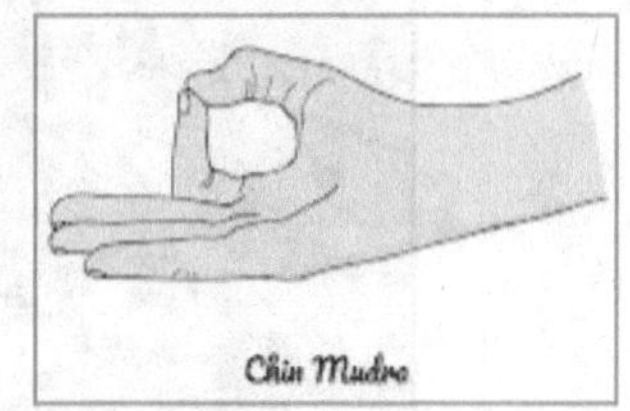

Śaṇkara's Dakshiṇāmoorthi Ashṭakam may be referred).

In 982nd name *Yonimudrā* has been mentioned. The teacher has to be bowed with this signet. In *Navāvarṇa* worship also at the end of every *Āvarṇa*, *Śrī Devī* has to be bowed with this signet. This signet also indicates the unison of *Brahmam*—soul.

Each signet has to be shown by using all the fingers of both the hands and having them jointly in equal position. It has been mentioned that the five fingers of each hand indicate the five primary elements (earth, etc.), the right side and the right hand indicate the bright *Shiva* form and the left side and the left hand indicate the immaculate *Shakti* form. (It can be reminded that the left of the *Ardhanāree* is female form). While showing the signets by joining the hands, the unified form of *Shiva* and *Shakti* has to be imagined and the signets indicate the creation and other actions. It has been told that if the signets are shown properly the deities get satisfied else, they get angry.

Some more mudras – examples;

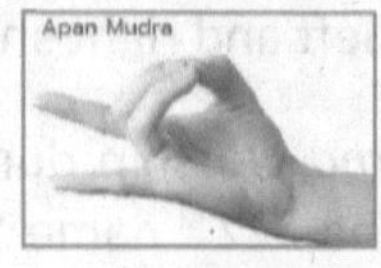

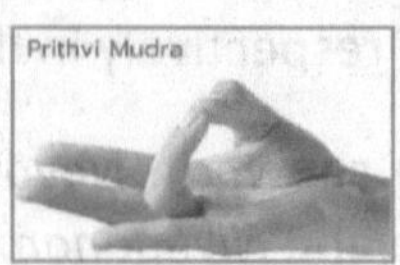

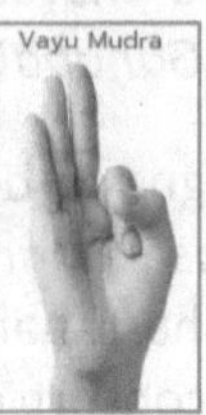

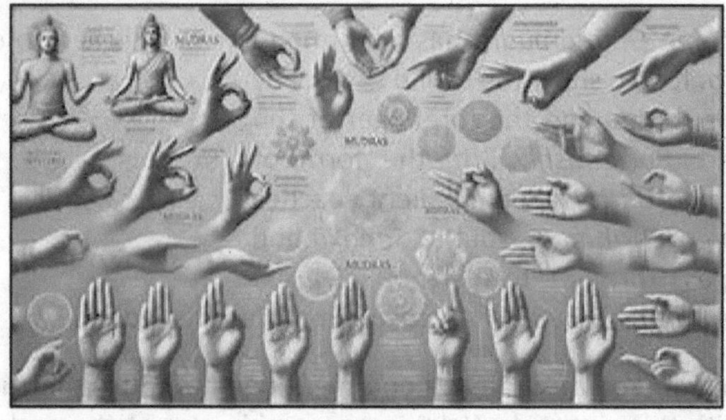

*****

Āvarṇams – An Overview

For the word *Āvarṇam*, we can have the meaning as curtain or enclosure. Worshipping till all the curtains are removed is called *Navāvarṇa* pooja. The 43 triangles have been discussed earlier. Now let us look at the same in a different perspective;

- 9 *Śaktis* – *Icchā, Kriyā, Gnāna, Satva, Rajas, Tamas, Paśyanti*[20], *Madyamā* and *Vaikharī*
- 10 organs – 5 organs of action, Mouth, Feet, Hands, Anus and *Upastam*.
- 5 organs of knowledge – Eyes, Nose, Mouth, Ears and Skin
- 5 *prāṇans* – *Prāṇan Apānan, Vyānan, Udānan* and *Samānan*
- 5 *karāṇas* – mind, intellect, haughty and will
- 5 elements of nature – Ether, Air, Fire, Water and Earth
- 10 sensitivities – sound, touching, form, smell, speech, *gamanam*, rhythm, *vasarggam* and bliss

It is customary to seek permission from the respective *Chakreshwari*s (Goddess presiding over the enclosure) before commencing any *Avarana* (enclosure) worship. The *Moola Mantra* (root mantra) is of paramount importance within these enclosures. When performing the ritual using a drawn *Sri Chakra*, it is considered most appropriate to keep the four gateways open; performing the ritual with the gateways closed—a practice followed in some *Yantras*—is not considered ideal. Specific colours are prescribed for each *Avarana* and the *Pancha Puja* (five-fold worship) must be offered to the respective *Chakreshwari*.

In many instances, the Sri Chakra is extolled more highly than Maha Meru. The nine enclosures represent the stages of a spiritual aspirant's journey—spanning the waking, dreaming and deep-sleep states, as well as the worship of the Supreme Lord, approaching the Guru, listening to his teachings (*Shravana*), reflection (*Manana*), profound contemplation (*Nitithyasana*) and the states of *Savikalpa* and *Nirvikalpa Samadhis*. These correspond respectively to the Bhupuras, the eight-petaled lotus, the sixteen-petaled lotus and so forth. These stages are common to both the unenlightened and the enlightened.

---

[20] 368th, 370th and 371st names in *Śrī Lalitā Sahasranāma* – *Paśyanti, Madyamā* and *Vaikharīrūpā*

Worship of the Supreme Lord (Ishvara), approaching the Guru, listening to sacred teachings (*Shravana*), contemplation (*Manana*) and the practices of *Bahirdashara* and *Antardashara* constitute the mature stages known as the eighth and ninth *Avaranas* (enclosures). The scriptures state that one can attain a sublime state simply by performing Puja for the seventh, eighth and the ninth *Avaranas* alone. The stage situated between the seventh and eighth *Avaranas* is where the Guru initiates the disciple. It is the Guru—who abides in *Nirvikalpa Samadhi*—imparts the appropriate form of worship to the disciple while in *Savikalpa Samadhi*. Thus, *Ayudha Puja* (worshipping the weapons) is performed at the eighth *Avarana*. The *Sri Lalita Sahasranama* names "*Krodhākārāṅ Kuśojjvalā*" (9) and "*Manorūpekṣu Kodaṇḍā*" (10) elucidate the necessity and significance of *Ayudha Puja*.

Lord *Viṣṇu* is present in a *Saḷagrāma*, Lord *Śiva* is present in a *Linga* and in the same way *Śrī Devī* is present is *Śrī Chakra*. Squares, circles, triangles and petals are all seen in a *Śrī Chakra*. Since it has nine *Chakras*, it is called *Navayoni Chakram*. Since it has 43 triangles it is called *tricatvārimśad Chakra*. *Śrī Devī's mātrukā śaktis* are present in this Chakra and hence it is called as *Mātrukā Chakram*. It is also called in tantras as *Parama Maṅgaḷa Chakram*, *Śivaśakti Aikya Chakram*, *Sadānanda Sampūrna Chakram* and so on. It has to be kept in the heart, called as *Daharākāśam* and worshipped.

1. First *Āvarṇam* – to integrate
2. Second *Āvarṇam* – to complete
3. Third *Āvarṇam* – to get excited
4. Fourth *Āvarṇam* – to approach/ access
5. Fifth *Āvarṇam* – to carry out
6. Sixth *Āvarṇam* – to protect
7. Seventh *Āvarṇam* – to cleanse
8. Eighth *Āvarṇam* – to accomplish
9. Ninth *Āvarṇam* – to create

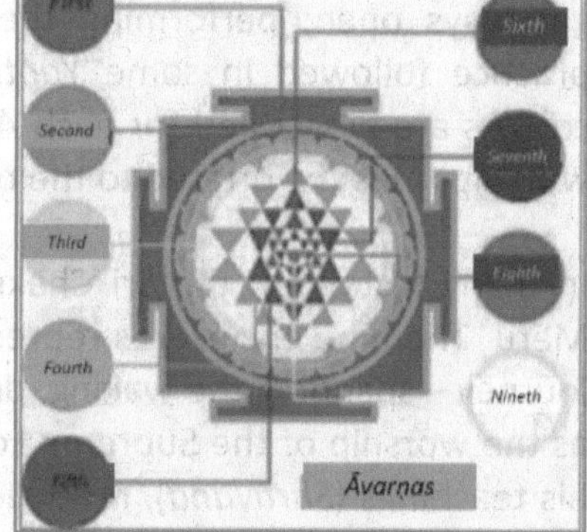

The details of all the nine *Āvarṇa*-s are summarized in this table;

Eighth	Seventh	Sixth	Fifth	Fourth	Third	Second	First	*Āvarṇam*
Sarva Siddhi	*Sarva Roga Hara*	*Sarva Rakśārkara*	*Sarvārtthā Sādakam*	*Sarva Soubhāgya*	*Sarva Sankśobaṇa*	*Sarvāśā Paripūraka*	*Trailokya Mohanam*	*Chakram*
Triangle	8 Triangles	10 Triangles	10 Triangles	14 Triangles	8 petals	16 petals	*Bhūpuram* with three	Form
Tripurāmbā	*Tripura Siddhā*	*Tripura Mālinī*	*Tripurāśrī:*	*Tripura Vāsinī*	*Tripura Sundarī*	*Tripureśī*	*Tripurā*	*Cakreśwari*
Hsraim Hsklrīm Hsrou:	*Hrīm Śrīm Sou:*	*Hrīm Klīm Blem*	*Hsaim Hsklīm*	*Haim Hklīm Hsou:*	*Hrīm Klīm Sou:*	*Aim Klīm Sou:*	*Am Ām Sou:*	*Mantram*
Icchā	*Buddhi*	*Prakāmya*	*Vaṣitva*	*Īṣitva*	*Mahimā*	*Laghimā*	*Aṇimā*	*Siddhi*
Sarva Bīja	*Sarva Keśarī*	*Sarva Mahānkuśā*	*Sarvonmādini*	*Sarva Vaśankarī*	*Sarvākarṣiṇī*	*Sarva Vidrāviṇi*	*Sarva Samkśobiṇī*	*Mudrā*
Gam	*Gam*	*Ram*	*Em*	*Īm*	*Ham*	*Sam*	*Lam*	*Bīja*
Plumeria (*Bandūka*) flower	Sapphire stone	Hibiscus flower		Pomegranate fruit	Hibiscus flower	White	White, Red, Yellow	Colour
Athirahasya	*Rahasya*	*Nigarba*	*Kulottīrṇa*	*Sampradāya*	*Gupta Tara*	*Gupta*	*Prakaṭa*	*Chitśakti Yoginī*

Āvarṇam	*Chakram*	Form	*Cakreśwari*	*Mantram*	*Siddhi*	*Mudrā*	*Bīja*	Colour	*Chitśakti Yoginī*	
Ninth	*Sarvānand amaya*	Dot	*Mahā Tripura*	*Pancadaśi*		*Sarva Kāma Siddhi & Sarva Trikaṇḍā*	*Hrīm*		*Parā Parādhi Rahasya*	

Step by step, crossing all the nine *Āvarṇas*, *Bindu* – unison of *Śiva-Śakti* – the liberation – the super bliss, can be reached. In each of the *Āvarṇas*, *Śrī Devī* is worshipped alongwith her *Āvarṇa Devīs* and at the end of the pooja, *Śrī Devī* is worshipped at *Bindu* and reach the happiness. This is *Navāvarṇa* pooja. In each of the *Āvarṇas*, the concerned *Cakreśwari*, *Mudrā Devī* and other *Āvarṇa Devīs* should be worshipped as prescribed and recommended. Only after their permission, the devotee can step into the next *Āvarṇa*. Only by this method, the devotee reaching the *Bindu*, *Śrī Devī* becomes happy and satiated.

Śrī Chakra Navāvarṇa pooja is considered as a *mahā yagnam*. An enthusiast performing this pooja with devotion gets multi-times benefit than performing *mahā* yagnas like *Vājabeyam*, *Somayāgam*, *Aśvametam*, etc. *Śrī Devī* gets much pleased and bestows her full compassion on this devotee. 230th name in *Śrī Lalitā Sahasranāma* – *Mahā Yāga Kramārādhyā* is worth noting here.

When a beneficiary enters the region, he is getting rid of the world's distractions and conflicts. With more icons and scenes, he is taken to a separate world. Bindu refers to the meeting of the universe called our body and its inherent source.

Sri Devi Bhagavatam 12th *Skandam*, chapters 10 to 12 describe the Manidveepam the dwelling place of *Sri Devi*. These 9 *Āvarṇa*-s are metamorphically compared to the 9 halls made of nine-gems (each with one gem). These 9 halls are mentioned as surrounding the *Chintamani* house – There lives *Sri Devi*. All the *Āvarṇa Devis* detailed below are explained in those chapters.

__Pañca Pañcikā Pooja__ – Upon completion of *Navāvarṇa pooja* in all the nine *āvaraṇas*, it has to be imagined on the dot, *Bindu* as; There are five faculties that have been placed on top of each other in the form of a *Simhāsana* (throne in the form of a lion) – five *Devīs* have to be imagined in the north-east, north-west, south-east and south-west corners and in the middle – such an imaginative pooja is called *Pañca Pañcikā Pooja*. These stages indicate the top most levels of meditation – Samprajnata

Samadhi. They are called *Sāmyam, Layam, Vināśam* and *Atyantara Bhāva Aikyam.*

__Ṣaḍhādhaara Pooja__ – In all the six sources starting from *Mūlādhāram* – identifying the six energies of *Gaṇapati, Brahmā, Viṣṇu, Rudran,* Soul and *Paramātmā* in the forms of *Sākinī, Kākinī, Lākinī, Rākinī, Ḍāknī* and *Hākinī* is *Ṣaḍhādhaara Pooja.* During this worship, it has to be sensed that all these are the forms of *Parāśakti* only. That is *Ṣaḍhādhaara*

Pooja. Along with this it has to be sensed that *Śrī Devī* is seated in all the *grantis* in the middle of the *Chakras.*

__Āmnāya Samaṣṭi pooja__ –

- East – *Rig Veda* – *Śuddha Vidyā*, chief of the 24,000 deities, *Bālā Dvādaśārddhā* and *Matanginī* are all permanently reside here.
- South – *Yajur Veda* – *Sowbhāgya Vidyā*, chief of the 36,000 deities, *Bagalā, Vārāhi, Vaṭukapriyā* and *Traskarinī* are all permanently reside here.
- West – *Atarva Veda* – *Lopāmudrā*, chief of the 3,000 deities, *Kāmakalā* and *Annapūraṇi* are all permanently reside here.

- North – *Sāma Veda* – *Śāmbavī Vidyā*, chief of the 2,000 deities, *Turyāmbā*, *Mahārddhā*, *Aśvārūḍā*, *Miśrāmbā* and *Vāgvādinī* are all permanently reside here.
- Along with these upwards – *Upaniṣad*
- Downwards – *Upaniṣads* as goal imaginative
- *Gaṇapati* in the South-west corner
- Sun in the North-west corner
- *Agni* (fire) in the North-east corner
- *Śiva* in the South-east corner

All the six *Āmnāyas* include seven crores of *mantras*. All the mantras reflect *Chitśaktis*. One has to worship realizing all these and that is *Āmnāya Samaṣṭi pooja*.

First *Āvarṇam*

The first enclosure is characterized by the syllable *'La'* and is associated with the colours red, white and yellow. It encompasses, the *Ashta Matrukas* (starting with *Brahmi*), the *Mudra* deities (who bestow bliss and other boons) and the deities of the *Siddhis* (such as *Anima*); all of these exist within the awakrning state (*Jagrat Avastha*). The *Anima Siddhi* signifies the gross body (*Sthoola*) and *Vishva*, is the *Devata*, the consciousness presiding over it. This enclosure is known as the *Trailokya Mohana Chakra*. The three concentric lines here constitute this first enclosure. The presiding deity (*Chakreshvari*) of this group—collectively known as the *Prakata Yoginis*—is referred to as *Tripura Chakreshvari*. Arranged across the three lines—coloured white, red and yellow, respectively—are the *Siddhi* deities (starting with *Anima*), the *Matrukas* (starting with *Brahmi*) and the *Mudra* deities (starting with *Sarva-samkshobhini*).

Many sages have attained all the eight Siddhis (beginning with *Anima*) through the worship of this *Chakreshvari*. The first Avarana (enclosure) alone suffices; the deities of this *Bhupura-traya* (three lines) possess the power to bestow omnipotence upon the *Jeeva* (individual soul) at the very outset. The state of the *Jeeva* in this first *Avarana* is likened to the exalted state of the sages who have attained mastery over the entire universe through the *Bala Mantra*. Thus, the truth that the beginning is indeed the end becomes as clear as a gooseberry held in the palm of one's hand. As the *Jeeva*—situated in this first Avarana—turns its gaze inward, it gains mastery over the *Sthoola* (gross), *Sookshma* (subtle) and *Karana* (causal) bodies. When these three bodies are captivated by the *Atman* (Self), nothing remains but the *Atman* itself; this represents the state of absolute solitude (*Ekanta*) symbolised by the *Bindu*. Here, the practice of *Nitithyasana*—remaining solitary even while surrounded by a multitude—is cultivated. The deities of this *Avarana* are known as *Prakata Yoginis* (Manifest Yoginis); the name is fitting, as they reveal the seeker's own inner nature to the seeker themselves.

The *Bhūpuram* with three squares is the first *Āvarṇam*. There are variances in the shape of the *Bhūpuras* as shown in the picture.

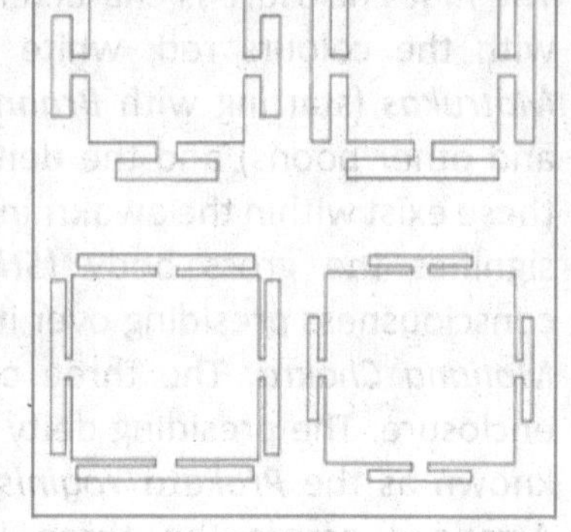

- This *Chakra* is called as "*Trailokya Mohanam*", meaning fascinating all the three worlds.
- The *Cakreśwari* of this *Āvarṇam* is *Tripurā*[21]. She has and she bestows all *Siddhis*.
- The *mantra* of this *Āvarṇam* is "*Am Ām Sou: Trailokya Mohana Cakrāya Nama:*".
- *Aṇimā Siddhi* and *Sarva Samkśobiṇī Mudrā*[22] are controlling this *Āvarṇam*.
- Its *bīja* letter is '*Lam*', that of the earth.
- Hence this *Chakra* has the characteristics of the Earth. So, the name of the *Chitśakti* in this *Chakra* is "*Prakaṭa Yoginī*".
- Everything perceivable and the comforts wherein, during awaken status of the physical body, the knowledge organs and mind are all indicated by this *Āvarṇam*.
- There are 3 lines around the *Chakra*. The *Siddhi Devīs*[23] are seated in the first line, 8 mothers (*Aṣṭa Mātās*) in the second and Mudrā Devīs in the third.
- The colour of the first line is white, the second is red and the third is yellow.

The *Siddhi Devīs* in the first line are – 1. *Aṇimā Siddhi*, 2. *Laghimā Siddhi*, 3. *Mahimā Siddhi*, 4. *Īṣitva Siddhi*, 5. *Vaṣitva Siddhi*, 6. *Prākāmya Siddhi*, 7. *Buddhi Siddhi*, 8. *Icchā Siddhi*, 9. *Prāpti Siddhi* and 10. *Sarva Kāma Siddhi* or *Mokśa Siddhi*.

---

[21] 626th name in *Śrī Lalitā Sahasranāma – Tripurā – त्रिपुरा*

[22] Mudra or mudrai is a hand signet or a symbol of bliss.

[23] *Siddhi* is the task of focused mind.

The first line is known as *Divyougham*. It pertains to the realm of the mind—specifically the nature of the form of *Pramatru Chaitanya* (the consciousness of the knower)—where the mind is the primary factor. For this very reason, the *Divyougha* Guru is venerated first among the Gurus. It is through this *Divyougha* Guru that the *Adi Guru* (Primal Guru) is revealed to us; without this, the grandeur of the lineage and the profound essence of *Sri Vidya* would remain beyond human grasp. The mind is inherently restless; yet, for one who engages in *Atma-vichara* (self-inquiry) within the mind itself—seeking the Supreme Non-dual Reality (*Paramadvaita*) through a mind steeped in the *Mantra*—external objects hold no utility. Here, the *Adi Guru* manifests as the Supreme Illumination (*Para-prakasha*).

The 8 mothers in the second line are – 1. *Brāhmi*, 2. *Māheśwari*, 3. *Koumāri*, 4. *Vaiṣṇavi*, 5. *Vārāhi*, 6. *Māhendri*, 7. *Cāmuṇḍā* and 8. *Mahālakśmi*.

The second line is known as *Siddhougham*. It is characterized by the dominance of the senses. It represents *Pramana-chaitanyam* (consciousness associated with the means of valid knowledge).

The *Devīs*[24] in the third line are – 1. *Sarva Samkśobiṇi*, 2. *Sarva Vidrāviṇi*, 3. *Sarva Ākarṣiṇi*, 4. *Sarva Vaśaṅkari*, 5. *Sarva Unmādini*, 6. *Sarva Mahāvruśā*, 7. *Sarva Keśari*, 8. *Sarva Bījā*, 9. *Sarva Yoni* and 10. *Sarva Trikaṇḍā*.

The third line is known as *Manavougham*. It pertains to *Prameya-Chaitanya* — the contemplation of the gross universe.

If a devotee worship *Śrī Devī*, controlling his organs, then definitely, he will be removed of all his sins and will get rid of six (internal) enemies of the mind, which are – *kāma* (lust), *krodha* (anger), *lobha* (greed), *moha* (attachment), *mada* (pride) and *mātsarya* (jealousy) – the negative characteristics which prevent man from attaining *mokśa* or salvation. If *Śrī Devī* is worshipped with devotion in this *Āvarṇam*, the devotee will be blessed with all the *Siddhis*.

---

[24] The names of these *Devīs* can be read in further chapters on *Khadgamāla Stotra*.

In this *Āvarṇam*, there are doors[25] on all the four sides. These are in the form *Rig*, *Yajur*, *Sāma* and *Atharva Vedas*. The philosophy behind is that only through *Vedas*, *Śrī Devī* can be attained.

The six *Chakras*, *Mūlādhāra*, *Svādhiṣṭāna*, *Maṇipūraka*, *Anāhata*, *Viśuddhi* and *Ajñā*, alongwith *Brahmarandiram*, the *Gula Sahasrāram* (beneath the *Mūlādhāra*), the *Agula Sahasrāram* (above the *Mūlādhāra*) and the inner tongue – totaling 10 *Mudrā Devīs* and crores of *Devī*, worship *Śrī Devī* in this *Āvarṇam*. Their names are – *Rasa Siddhi, Mokśa Siddhi, Pala Siddhi, Khadka Siddhi, Pādukā Siddhi, Añjana Siddhi, Vāg Siddhi, Loka Siddhi* and *Deha Siddhi*. They are all in the form beautiful young girls of 16 years age. They bless the worshipper and send him to the next stage.

Śrī Muthuswamy Dīkṣitar has lyricized nine songs called, "*Kamalāmba Navāvarṇa*" songs. The song pertaining to this *Āvarṇa* begins with "*Kamalāmba Samrakśatu Mām (Śrī) Hruṭ*".

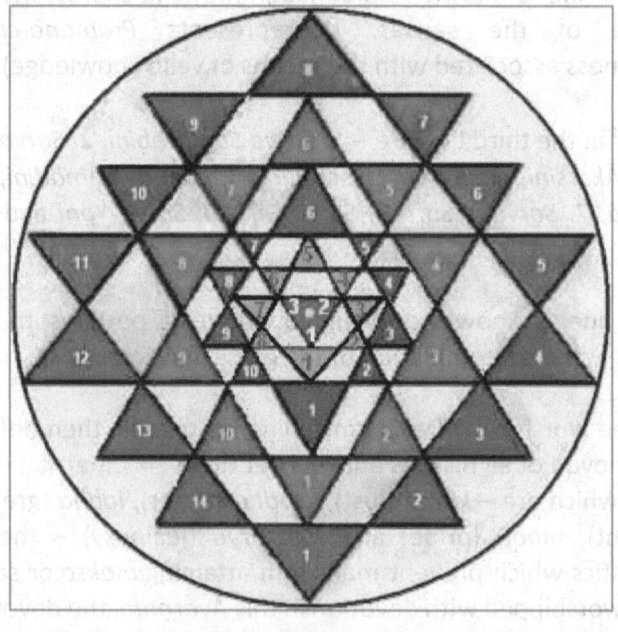

*****

---

[25] These doors have been discussed earlier.

Second *Āvarṇam*

The second Avarana (enclosure) is characterized by the letter *'La'* (*Lakara-prakriti*) and is white in colour. It embodies the nature of the Moon, encompassing all sixteen of the Moon's phases (*Kalas*). Due to this lunar association, this *Avarana* signifies the *Swapna* (dream) state. In the dream state, the mind alone holds sway; the sensory organs remain motionless and the mind reigns supreme. Consequently, everything perceived within

the dream is a manifestation of the mind. The very act of recounting a dream reflects the mind's inward focus. At this stage, the mind attains the quality of *Shuddha Sattva* (pure luminosity/ goodness); hence, the colour white is attributed to it. The presiding deities associated with this *Avarana* are *Hiranyagarbha* and *Taijasa*, corresponding respectively to the gross (*Sthoola*) and subtle (*Sookshma*) aspects of existence.

The presiding deity of this Avarana (enclosure) is <u>Sarvasa-paripuraka Chakreshvari</u>; its *Siddhi* deity is *Laghima Siddhi* and its *Mudra* deity is *Sarva-vidravini*. This *Chakreshvari* represents Artha (Economy). *Artha* can be understood as 'meaning' or 'substance' and the term also signifies wealth. Just as a word and its meaning are inseparable, one's actions must align with *Dharma* (righteousness); indeed, wealth acquired in accordance with *Dharma* is the only kind that holds true significance. In this *Avarana*, what is signified by *Artha* refers to the mental modifications (*Vruttis*) that articulate meaning. These must be meaningful and substantial, yet simultaneously remain bound by the principles of *Sri Vidya Dharma*.

The second *Āvarṇam* has 16 petals – five *prāṇas*, 5 knowledge organs, 5 organs of action and the mind.

- This *Chakra* is called as "*Sarvāśā Paripūrakam*".
- The *Cakreśwari* of this *Āvarṇam* is *Tripureśī*.
- The *mantra* of this *Āvarṇam* is "*Aim Klīm Sou: Sarvāśā Paripūraka Cakrāya Nama:*".
- *Laghimā Siddhi* and *Sarva Vidrāvini Mudrā* are controlling this *Āvarṇam*.
- Its *bīja* letter is '*Sam*', that of the Moon.
- The colour of this *Āvarṇam* is white.
- The name of the *Chitśakti* in this *Chakra* is "*Gupta Yoginī*".

There used to be three states of mind – awakened, sleep and deep sleep. (*Jāgrath*, *Swapna* and *Śuṣupti*). The previous *Āvarṇam* was related to awakened (*Jāgrath*) state and this *Āvarṇam* is being related to sleep (*Swapna*) state. This *Āvarṇam* indicates the subtle body and the status of mind during sleep. The sleeping state originates in the neck and hence the 16 petalled *Viśuddhi Chakra* in the neck. That is the 16 petalled second *Āvarṇam*. *Chitśakti* is in-charge of this. The 16 *Gupta Yoginīs*[26] in this *Chakra* make all the 8 directions happy by spreading the nectar. Their names are; 1. *Kāma Ākarṣiṇi*, 2. *Buddhi Ākarṣiṇi*, 3. *Ahaṅkāra Ākarṣiṇi*, 4. *Śabda Ākarṣiṇi*, 5. *Sparśa Ākarṣiṇi*, 6. *Rūpa Ākarṣiṇi*, 7. *Rasa Ākarṣiṇi*, 8. *Ganda Ākarṣiṇi*, 9. *Siddha Ākarṣiṇi*, 10. *Dairya Ākarṣiṇi*, 11. *Smrutya Ākarṣiṇi*, 12. *Nāma Ākarṣiṇi*, 13. *Bīja Ākarṣiṇi*, 14. *Ātma Ākarṣiṇi*, 15. *Amruta Ākarṣiṇi* and 16. *Śarīra Ākarṣiṇi*

The 15 items viz., Ether, Air, Fire, Water, Earth, *Srotram*, *Tvakś*, *Cakśush*, Tongue, *Kāraṇam*, Speech, Style, Feet, Gas and *Upastam* alongwith clumsy mood are directed in the right path by the above 16 *Gupta Yoginīs* by sitting in the 16 petalled lotus.

---

[26] It is told that there 64 crores of *Yoginīs* – 237th name in *Śrī Lalitā Sahasranāma* – *Mahācatuṣṣaṣṭi-koṭi yogini gaṇa sevitā* – महाचतुष्षष्टि कोटि योगिनी गनसेविता

The *Navāvarṇa* song of *Śrī Muthuswamy Dīkṣitar* pertaining to this *Āvarṇa* begins with *"Kamalāmbām Baja Re Re Mānasa"*.

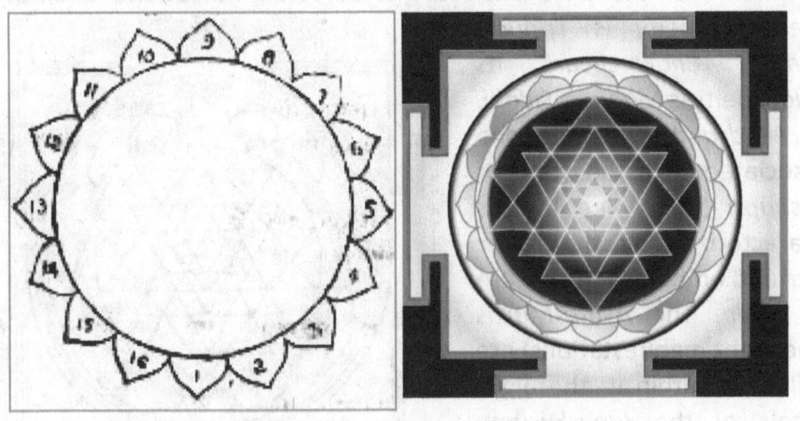

*****

Third *Āvarṇam*

The name of the third enclosure is *Sarva-Sankshobhana Chakra*. Its presiding deity is *Tripura-Sundari Chakreshvari*. Its *Siddhi* deity is *Mahima-Siddhi*. Its *Mudra* deity is the one associated with the state of *Sushupti* (deep sleep). It is characterized by the letter '*Ha*' and embodies the nature of *Shiva*. The *Ashta-Murtis* (the eight manifestations) are reflected within it; the eight petals of the *Japa-kusuma* (hibiscus) flower symbolize these *Ashta-Murtis*. These

eight manifestations are: *Prakruti, Mahat, Ahamkara*, the five *Tanmatras* (subtle elements), the five *Bhutas* (gross elements), the *Jnanendriyas* and *Karmendriyas* (organs of perception and action), the *Antahkarana-Chatushtaya* (the four internal faculties) and *Purusha* (the Conscious Self), who is the master of them all. This aspect is referred to as the *Antaryami* (Inner Controller) and Prajna in relation to the *Karana-Sarira* (Causal Body).

The third *Āvarṇam* has 8 petals – *Mahat* philosophy, the haughty, the five souls, the five base elements, the five sense organs and the soul are the eight petals of this *Āvarṇam*.

- This *Chakra* is called as "*Sarva Saṅkṣobaṇam*".
- The *Cakreśwari* of this *Āvarṇam* is *Tripura Sundarī*[27].
- The *mantra* of this *Āvarṇam* is "*Hrīm Klīm Sou: Sarva Saṅkṣobaṇa Cakrāya Nama:*".
- *Mahimā Siddhi* and *Sarvākarṣiṇī Mudrā* are controlling this *Āvarṇam*.
- Its *bīja* letter is '*Ham*', that of the *Śiva*.
- The colour of this *Āvarṇam* is the colour of hibiscus flower.
- The name of the *Chitśakti* in this *Chakra* is "*Gupta Tara Yoginī*".

---

[27] 234th name in *Śrī Lalitā Sahasranāma – Mahā Tripurasundarī –* महात्रिपुरसुन्दरी

This *Āvarṇam* is being related to third state of mind i.e., deep sleep (*Śuṣupti*) state. The *Śuṣupti* state is called daily great dissolution. This *Āvarṇam* indicates the sufferings and enjoyments of the physical body and mind, during the *Śuṣupti* state.

The 8 *Gupta Tara Yoginīs* in this *Chakra* make all the 8 directions happy by spreading the nectar. Their names are; 1. *Ananga Kusumā*, 2. *Ananga Mekalā*, 3. *Ananga Madanā*, 4. *Ananga Madanā Turā*, 5. *Ananga Rekhā*, 6. *Ananga Veginā*, 7. *Ananga Anguśā* and 8. *Ananga Malinī*. They have a very terrific form and have very serious eye-sight. They have crores of entourage.

The *Navāvarṇa* song of *Śrī Muthuswamy Dīkṣitar* pertaining to this *Āvarṇa* begins with "*Śrī Kamalāmbikayā Kaṭākṣitosham*".

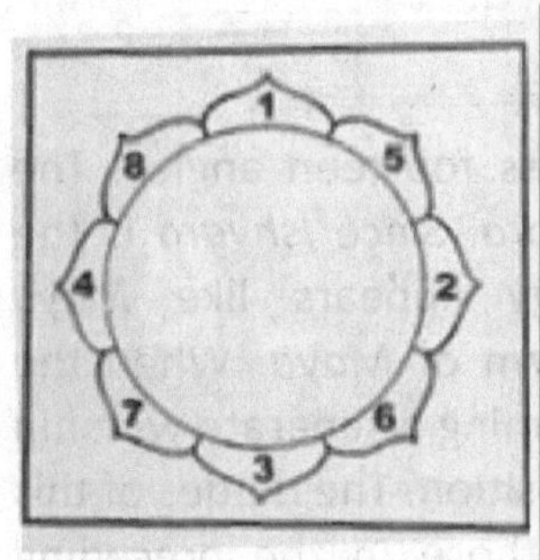

*****

Fourth *Āvarṇam*

The name of the fourth *Avarana* (enclosure) is *Sarva Saubhagya Dayaka Chakra*. Its presiding deity is *Tripuravasini Chakreshvari*. Its *Siddhi* deity is *Īshitva Siddhi*. Its *Mudra* deity is *Sarva Vashankari*. It takes the *Tureeya* (fourth-transcendental) sound *'Eem'* as its *Prakruti* (fundamental nature). The *Kamakala Beeja* known as *'Eem'* encompasses the fourteen worlds within itself. It resembles the colour of a pomegranate flower. The

deities of this enclosure are worshipped across fourteen angles. The fourth enclosure signifies the worship of *Ishvara*. Since *Ishvara* is the universe itself—and because cosmic energy appears like *Maya* (illusion)—the worship of *Ishvara* is also a form of *Maya*. When the universe is identified as *Lalita*, the act of performing a separate worship for it, reflects the state of our own mental disposition. The deities of this enclosure manifest in the same manner as those in the preceding enclosures.

The word *Shobhanam* often carries the connotation of agitation or turbulence. It is the mind that becomes agitated. The fear arising in the mind and the attachment to objects are both impulses, driven by the mind itself. To dispel these, one requires an anchor or a support. Whenever a sense of fear arises, one seeks a companion. That companion is found within through *Ishvara*—manifesting as the realisation of "*Saha aham-Soham*" (I am He). The guidance received from this *Ishvara* is referred to by various names, such as *Antaryami* (the Inner Controller) or conscience. The *Sarvakarshini* (All-Attracting) *Shakti* represents the development of attachment towards that *Ishvara*.

The fourth *Āvarṇam* has 14 triangles.

- This *Chakra* is called as "*Sarva Soubhāgya Dhāyakam*".
- The *Cakreśwari* of this *Āvarṇam* is *Tripura Vāsinī*.
- The *mantra* of this *Āvarṇam* is "*Haim Hklīm Hsou: Sarva Soubhāgya Dhāyaka Cakrāya Nama:*".
- *Īṣitva Siddhi* and *Sarva Vaśaṅkarī Mudrā* are controlling this *Āvarṇam*.
- Its *bīja* letter is '*Īm*', that of the great illusion (*Mahā Māyā*).
- The colour of this *Āvarṇam* is the that of pomegranate fruit.
- The name of the *Chitśakti* in this *Chakra* is "*Sampradāya Yoginī*".

Śrī Parameśwaran, himself or through *Gurus* bestows wisdom and hence this is '*Sampradāyam*'.

Śrī Parameśwaran is the earliest *Guru* and the cause of this whole universe. This *Āvarṇam* indicates, he being present in all the 14 worlds. The philosophy of this *Āvarṇam* is that realizing that the *Chitśakti* is beyond the triplet the knower, the known and the knowledge.
The 14 *Sampradāya Yoginīs* in this *Chakra* are; 1. *Sarva Saṅkśobiṇi*, 2. *Sarva Vidrāviṇi*, 3. *Sarvākarṣiṇi*, 4. *Sarvāhlādini*, 5. *Sarva Sammohini*, 6. *Sarva Stambini*, 7. *Sarva Jrumbini*, 8. *Sarva Vaśaṅkari*, 9. *Sarva Ranjani*, 10. *Sarvonmādini*, 11. *Sarvārthasādini*, 12. *Sarva Sampatthi Pūrani*, 13. *Sarva Mantramayī* and 14. *Sarva Dvandva Kśayaṅkari*.

The 14 *nādi* energies viz., *Alambusā, Guhā, Viśvodari, Vāraṇā, Hasti, Jihvā, Yaśovati, Bayaśvini, Kāntāri, Pūṣā, Śangini, Sarasvati, Iḍā, Pingaḷā* and *Śuṣumnā* are these *Yoginīs*.

The *Navāvarṇa* song of *Śrī Muthuswamy Dīkṣitar* pertaining to this *Āvarṇa* begins with "*Śrī Kamalāmbikāyai Kanakāmśukāyai*".

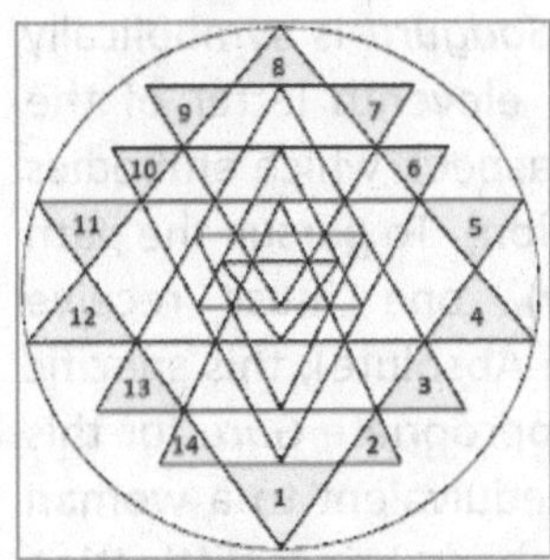

*****

Fifth *Āvarṇam*

The name of the fifth Avarana (enclosure) is *Sarvartha Sadhaka Chakra*. Its presiding deity is *Tripura Sri Chakreshwari*. The deity of its *Siddhi* (attainment) is *Vashitva Siddhi* and its *Mudra* deity is *Sarvonmadini*. It is grounded in the syllable *'Aem'*. In the ten outer angles of the *Bahirdashara*, the presiding deities rule as manifestations of Vishnu, who enacted the *Dashavatara* (ten incarnations). These deities are depicted as having a  vermilion hue. This *Avarana* signifies the approach to the *Guru*. It represents the Divine (*Ishvara*)—whose nature was described in the fourth Avarana—assuming a human form as part of His divine play (*Leela*). Vishnu's ten incarnations explicitly illustrate the Divine manifesting in the form of a *Guru*. When the Divine remains concealed, the truth is not understood; this reflects the state of mind Arjuna experienced in the Mahabharata. Arjuna can be regarded as a representative of all disciples. Today, many disciples—beset by doubts and misconceptions—resemble Arjuna.

These are all explicitly realisible. Hence, the name *Bahirdashara* (Ten external manifestations). It is the duty of the *Sadguru* to impart *Brahma-jnana* (knowledge of the Absolute) to those who approach him while observing *Brahmacharya* (celibacy). Here, the *Sadguru* is symbolically represented by the letter *'Aem'* (Ae-kara), the eleventh letter of the alphabet; this signifies the *Ekadasha* (eleventh) aspect, which embodies the nature of the *Yoni* (the divine source of creation). To pursue the path of realising the Absolute (*Brahma-sadhana*), one must receive instructions in *Brahma-vidya* (the science of the Absolute); this specific layer of the teaching explains how to find the appropriate *Guru* for this purpose. Approaching the *Guru* is regarded as equivalent to a woman searching for her husband. Devotion to one's husband brings distinction to a virtuous woman, for he is considered equal to the Divine. Nature itself yields to the words of such a virtuous woman; disciples must approach and revere their *Guru* with a similar degree of reverence and purity. The underlying meaning is that, one should not contemplate any deity other than one's own *Guru*. The *Guru* embodies the form of *Ardhanarishvara* (the androgynous union of *Shiva* and *Shakti*). The esoteric significance of women applying vermilion (*sindhoor*) to the parting of their hair is explained in the *Sammohana Nyasa* ritual. Here, the Guru assumes the form of Lord Vishnu—the deity responsible for *Rakshana* (preservation)—among the cosmic functions of creation, preservation and dissolution. This is because none other than the Guru safeguards disciples, guiding them to adhere to the traditions and preventing them from straying into error.

The fifth *Āvarṇam* has 10 triangles.

- This *Chakra* is called as "*Sarvārttha Sādakam*".
- The *Cakreśwari* of this *Āvarṇam* is *Tripurāśrī:*.
- The *mantra* of this *Āvarṇam* is "*Hsaim Hsklīm Hsou: Sarvārttha Sādaka Cakrāya Nama:*".
- *Vaṣitva Siddhi* in the *Nāma Rūpa* form, which is the power of lust in the souls and *Sarvonmādini Mudrā*, indicating the madness to reach liberation, are controlling this *Āvarṇam*.
- Its *bīja* letter is '*Em*'.
- The name of the *Chitśakti* in this *Chakra* is "*Kulottīrṇa Yoginī*".

Kulam here is the heredity – heredity of *gurus*. *Uttīrṇa* means developing well. Hence the blessings of *Gurus* and the development of Guru-disciple race are the results of worshipping this *Āvarṇam*. Since this bestows all the economic needs of the devotees, this *Chakra* is called *Sarvārtthā Sādakam*. Worshipping *Śrī Devī* in the form of *Guru* is the significance of this *Āvarṇam*.

The 10 *Kulottīrṇa Yoginīs* in this *Chakra* are; 1. *Sarva Siddhi Pradhā*, 2. *Sarva Sampath Pradhā*, 3. *Sarva Priankari*, 4. *Sarva Maṅgala Kāriṇi*, 5. *Sarva Kāma Pradhā*, 6. *Sarva Dukkha Vimośani*, 7. *Sarva Mrutyu Praśamani*, 8. *Sarva Vigna Nivāriṇi*, 9. *Sarvāṅga Sundari* and 10. *Sarva Soubhāgya Dāyini*.

The 10 gases viz. – *Apānan, Vyānan, Udānan, Samānan, Nāgan, Kūrman, Girikaran, Devadattan* and *Danañjayan*, indicate the 10 triangles in this *Chakra*.

The *Navāvarṇa* song of *Śrī Muthuswamy Dīkṣitar* pertaining to this *Āvarṇa* begins with "*Śrī Kamalāmbāyā: Param Na Hi Re Re*".

*****

Sixth *Āvarṇam*

The name of the sixth enclosure is *Sarva Rakshakara Chakra*. Its presiding deity is *Tripura Malini*. Its *Siddhi* deity is *Prakamya Siddhi* and its *Mudra* deity is *Sarva Mahankusha*. It is characterised by the fire-syllable (*Agni-svara*) 'Ra'. The ten aspects (*Kalas*) of fire manifest here as the inner *Dashara* (ten-petaled). The radiance of this fire resembles the glowing, tender red hue of the *Japa-kusuma* (Hibiscus) flower.

This enclosure symbolises the initiation into the *mantra* (*Mantra Upadesha*) received through hearing. Initiation is not granted immediately upon approaching the *Guru*; the disciple must traverse several stages to attain it. A Guru accepts a disciple only after subjecting them to various tests. Only the disciple who shines like gold refined in fire through these trials is accepted as one worthy of the Guru's affection. When one accepts the *Guru's* true nature exactly as it is, the *Guru's* consciousness—manifesting as *Parahanta* (Supreme I-consciousness) and *Vimarsha* (Reflective Awareness)—fills the inner self; this state corresponds to a blend of white and red hues. Fire displays a unique colour resulting from the mingling of tender red at the top and a pale white at the base—a shade visible upon close inspection of a five-petaled hibiscus flower. It closely resembles the colour of sandalwood paste. In the worship of Sudha Devi, this blend is described as *Ashtagandha-lolita-pushpam* (a flower infused with the eight sacred fragrant pastes, including sandalwood and saffron).

This sixth *Āvarṇam* also has 10 triangles.

- This *Chakra* is called as "*Sarva Rakśārkara Chakram*".
- The *Cakreśwari* of this *Āvarṇam* is *Tripura Mālinī*.

- The *mantra* of this *Āvarṇam* is "*Hrīm Klīm Blem Sarva Rakṣārkara Cakrāya Nama:*".
- *Prakāmya Siddhi* and *Sarva Mahāṅkuśā Mudrā* are controlling this *Āvarṇam*.
- Its *bīja* letter is '*Ram*', that of *Agni* (fire).
- The colour of this *Āvarṇam* is the colour of hibiscus flower.
- The name of the *Chitśakti* in this *Chakra* is "*Nigarba Yoginī*". *Chitśakti* is secretly residing in the cave of the heart and hence this name.

Making the soul in its real form and again avoiding the fear on account duality – this *Chakra* protects from such fear and hence *Sarva Rakṣārkara Chakram*. The *Prakāmya Siddhi* is the extreme bliss, which is liked by everyone. *Sarva Mahāṅkuśā Mudrā* indicates the happiness got by the focused and concentrated prayer.

Śrī Devī is praised as "*Bahirmukha Sudurlabhā*" and "*Antarmukha Samā-rādhyā*". However, she has to be worshipped focused, continuous and concentrated mind (*Antarmukha*). That is the philosophy of worshipping in this *Āvarṇam*.

The 10 *Nigarba Yoginīs* in this *Chakra* are; 1. *Sarvajnā*, 2. *Sarva Śakti*, 3. *Sarvaiśvarya Pradhā*, 4. *Sarva Gnānamayi*, 5. *Sarva Vyādhi Nivārinī*, 6. *Sarvādhāra Swarūpā*, 7. *Sarva Pāpaharā*, 8. *Sarvānandamayī*, 9. *Sarva Rakṣā Swrūpiṇī* and 10. *Sarvepsita Phalapradā*.

The presiding *Śaktis* of these 10 triangles are the forms of *Agni* viz., - *Śokam, Pāśakam, Śośakam, Dāhakam, Plāvatam, Kśārakam, Utsārakam, Ceṣāpakam, Jarumpakam* and *Mohakam*.

The *Navāvarṇa* song of *Śrī Muthuswamy Dīkśitar* pertaining to this *Āvarṇa* begins with "*Śrī Kamalāmbikāyās Tava Baktoham*".

*****

Seventh *Āvarṇam*

The name of the seventh *Avarana* (enclosure) is *Sarva-roga-hara Chakra* (the circle that dispels all diseases). Its presiding deity is *Tripura-siddha* and the deity of its *Siddhi* (attainment) is *Buddhi-siddhi*. Its *Mudra* deity is *Sarva-kesari*. It is constituted by the *Matrukas* (the Samskruta alphabets) ranging from *'Am'* to *'Ksham'*. The syllable *'Ka'* signifies Brahman—*'Kam'* represents Brahman. The essence of *Kesari Mudra* lies in abiding in the nature of

Brahman; it signifies the spiritual practice wherein the mind—prone to doubt—attains the power of upward expansion (*Unmeelana Shakti*) towards the clear, expansive *Akasha* (ether/ consciousness).

These deities are described as embodying the *Ashta-murti* (the eight forms of Shiva) and the nature of *Kameshvara*, possessing a crimson hue resembling the *Padmaraga* (ruby) gemstone. The *Ashta-murti*s signify *Kameshvara*; indeed, Kameshvara is revealed to be present within all eight forms. To attain *Kameshvara*, the practice of *Mantra-sadhana*—specifically through the contemplation of the *Guru's* teachings—is essential. In this context, the constant contemplation of the Mantra is highly beneficial; hence, the *Matrukas* are mentioned here. *Padmaraga* is one of the *Navaratnas* (nine precious gems). While flowers were used as analogies in the preceding *Avaranas*, the Padmaraga gem-stone is cited here to signify a shift; whereas the first six *Avaranas* represented subtle emotional states, this seventh *Avarana* signifies unwavering mental resolve and steadfast faith in the doctrine that nothing exists in the world other than the *Guru*. All afflictions arising in the mind are classified as *Bhava-rogas* (diseases of worldly existence) and the *Sarva-roga-hara Chakra* serves to cure them. Here, the *Mantra*—manifesting as the *Guru's* word—is crucial; consequently, the *Vak-devatas* (deities of speech) are invoked and worshipped.

This seventh *Āvarṇam* has 8 triangles – iconic form of 8 gods (*Aṣṭa Mūrthis*).

- This *Chakra* is called as "*Sarva Roga Hara Chakram*".
- The *Cakreśwari* of this *Āvarṇam* is *Tripura Siddhā*.
- The *mantra* of this *Āvarṇam* is "*Hrīm Śrīm Sou: Sarva Roga Hara Cakrāya Nama:*".
- *Buddhi Siddhi* and *Sarva Keśarī Mudrā* are controlling this *Āvarṇam*.
- Its *bīja* letter is '*Gam*'.
- The colour of this *Āvarṇam* is the colour of sapphire precious stone.
- The name of the *Chitśakti* in this *Chakra* is "*Rahasya Yoginī*". *Chitśakti* is secretly residing in the cave of the heart and hence this name.

When it is said as '*Rogam*', everyone tends to think of disease in the body. The fact that the mental disease is the source for various ailments of the body, is entirely forgotten. Ignorance is the base for all illnesses. If it is removed, the mind and the body get cured. Hence this *Chakra* is called *Sarva Roga Hara Chakram*.

This *Chakra* is in the form of *Gnāna Bhūmika* (wisdom earth) called *Danumānasī*. The *Śaktis* of this *Chakra* are the *Mahā* (great) sentences initiated by the guru and repeated within the mind. The philosophy of pooja of this *Chakra* is the goal of *Mahā* (great) sentences viz. *Chitśakti* with *Śiva*.

The below mentioned 8 *Vaśinyādi Vāg Devīs* are the ones who scripted *Śrī Lalitā Sahasranāma*, as per the order of *Śrī Lalitā Devī*. Their dwelling place is this *Chakra*. They worship *Śrī Lalitā* through *Gadyam* (songs), *Padyam* (prose), *Kāvyam* (poem) and drama. To become expert in speech, the devotees worship *Sarasvatī Devī* in this *Chakra* with the mantra – Hrīm, Aim, Trīm, Glīm, Sou:

1. *Vaśini* – Vāg *Devī* with five letters in the '*ka*' series.
2. *Kāmeshi*
3. *Modini* – *Vāg Devī* with five letters in the '*ca*' series.
4. *Vimalā* – *Vāg Devī* with five letters in the '*ṭa*' series.
5. *Aruṇā* – *Vāg Devī* with five letters in the '*ta*' series.
6. *Jayinī* – *Vāg Devī* with five letters in the '*pa*' series.
7. *Sarveśvarī* – *Vāg Devī* with four letters '*ya*', '*ra*', '*la*' and '*va*'.

8.   *Koulini – Vāg Devī* with six letters '*sa*', '*ha*', '*śa*', '*ṣa*', '*kśa*' and '*Ja*'.

Eight secret *yonis* viz., chillness, heat, sorrow, lust, *Satvam*, *Rajas* and *Tamas*, are the *Śaktis* of the 8 triangles in this *Chakra*.

The *Navāvarṇa* song of *Śrī Muthuswamy Dīkśitar* pertaining to this *Āvarṇa* begins with "*Śrī Kamalāmbikāyām Baktim Karomi*".

*****

Eighth *Āvarṇam*

The worship of the weapons takes place prior to the eighth *Avarana* (enclosure) ritual. This specific worship—directed at the weapons situated outside the central *Tririkona* (triangle)—is known as Nididhyasana. Here, Nada (primordial sound) constitutes the fundamental nature (Prakruti) and the three *Gunas—Sattva*, *Rajas*, and *Tamas*—are paramount. The nature of the *Tri-Shakti* (the threefold power)— comprising *Iccha* (Will), *Kriya*

(Action) and *Jnana* (Knowledge)—is elucidated. The weapons, such as the five floral arrows (*Pancha Pushpa Bana*), embody the philosophical principles of the *Pancha Tanmatras* (the five subtle elements). The *Indra Dhanush* (Indra's Bow) signifies the mastery over the senses (*Indriyas*). The destruction of the *Pasa* (noose) and *Ankusa* (goad)—which represent the binding forces of *Vasana* (latent mental impressions)—is a crucial requirement for this *Upasana* (worship).

The name of the eighth *Avarana* is *Sarva Siddhiprada Chakra* (the Circle that Bestows All Accomplishments). Its presiding deity is *Tripuramba*; the deity of accomplishment (*Siddhi*) is *Iccha Siddhi*; and the deity of the *Mudra* (gesture) is *Sarvabeeja*.

This stage involves the unification of the three Avarana deities— *Kameshwari*, *Vajreshwari* and *Bhagamalini*—into the power of the Supreme *Brahmam* (Para-*Brahmam*). It signifies the dissolution of all things perceived in triads back into *Sri Devi*, who is the ultimate cause of the universe; these are the distinctive features of this *Avarana*. Worshipping this *Avarana* grants all accomplishments (*Sarva Siddhi*). As it is subtle/ secretive in nature, the presiding deity is known as *Ati-Rahasya Yogini* (the Supreme Secret Yogini).

This eighth *Āvarṇam* is one triangle.

- This *Chakra* is called as "*Sarva Siddhi Prata Chakram*".
- The *Cakreśwari* of this *Āvarṇam* is *Tripurāmbā*.
- The *mantra* of this *Āvarṇam* is "*Hsraim Hsklrīm Hsrou: Sarva Siddhi Prata Cakrāya Nama:*".
- *Icchā Siddhi* and *Sarva Bīja Mudrā* are controlling this *Āvarṇam*.
- Its *bīja* letter is '*Gam*'.
- The colour of this *Āvarṇam* is the colour of Plumeria (*Bandūka*) flower stone.
- The name of the *Chitśakti* in this *Chakra* is "*Athirahasya Yoginī*".

The soul mingling with the *Brahmam* is called *Sarva Siddhi*. That is the result and philosophy of worshipping this *Chakra*. This is possible only through daily meditation. That is why this is called *Sarva Siddhi Chakra*. The experience of realizing that everything originates only through the lust of *Chitśakti* is the *Icchā Siddhi*. *Chitśakti* is the seed for everything. The bliss obtained over realizing this through wisdom is the *Sarva Bīja Mudrā*. Such an imagination is the philosophy of this *Chakra*.

There are presiding deities for all weapons – noose, goad, sugar-cane bow and arrow are the weapons of *Śrī Devī*. Worshipping these weapons removes all the barriers of self-realization.

Totally there are 8 weapons – 4 belonging to *Kāmeśvara* and 4 belonging to *Kāmeśvarī*.

- *Agni chakram* in the *Kāmagiri Pīṭam* as *Icchā Śakti* as *Vāgīśvari* and *Brahma Ātma Śakti Kāmeśvarī*.
- *Sūrya chakram* in the *Pūrṇagiri Pīṭam* as *Gnāna Śakti* as *Kāmakalai* and *Viṣṇu Ātma Śakti Vajreśvarī*.
- *Soma chakram* in the *Jālantara Pīṭam* as *Kriyā Śakti* as *Parāparai* and *Rudra Ātma Śakti Bagamālinī*.

Avya tatvam, Mahat tatvam and haughty are the ones respectively in the forms of *Kāmeśvarī, Vajreśvarī* and *Bagamālinī*. This is the form of *Parabrahmam*.

The *Navāvarṇa* song of *Śrī Muthuswamy Dīkṣitar* pertaining to this *Āvarṇa* begins with "*Śrī Kamalāmbike sVāva Śive Karadruta Śikacārike*".

*****

Ninth *Āvarṇam*

The name of the ninth enclosure is the *Sarvanandamaya Chakra* (the Circle of All-Bliss). Its presiding deity is Sri *Lalita Maha Tripura Sundari.* Its deity of accomplishment (*Siddhi*) is *Sarva-Kama Siddhi* and its deity of Mudra is *Sarva-Trikhanda.*

Here, the *Moola Mantra*— either the *Panchadasee* or the *Shodasee*—is used for *Archana.* There are no separate deities for this enclosure; rather, the deities

of the enclosure are the very modifications (*vruttis*) of the inner instrument (*antahkarana*). *Lalita* is the One who exists both within the universe and transcends it, manifesting in the form of the *Mahameru* or *Sri Chakra* (which embodies the *Panchadasee* or *Shodasee* mantras). This sublime state is attained through the *Siddhi* known as *Prapti* (attainment). This is also the *Sarva-Yoni* (the Source of All). Only those who have practiced the various methods described thus far, and who have transcended the Turiya state to reach the state of pure consciousness (*Sanmaya*), can enter the *Sarvanandamaya Chakra.* There is nothing beyond it. This ninth enclosure is the Sarva-Purtikara Chakra (the Circle of Total Fulfillment). It signifies the seeker's arrival at a state devoid of the triad (*Tripudi*)—transcending the distinction between the knower (*Jnatru*), the knowledge (*Jnana*) and the object of knowledge (*Jneya*).

This is ninth and last *Āvarṇam* in the form of *Bindu*, a dot in the middle of the *Śrī Chakram.*

- This *Chakra* is called as "*Sarvānandamaya Chakram*".
- The *Cakreśwari* of this *Āvarṇam* is *Mahā Tripura Sundarī. Tripura Sundarī* in the form of *Śuṣupti* is the *Cakreśwari* of the third *Āvarṇam*

and *Tripura Sundarī* in the form of *Samādi* is the *Cakreśwari* of this *Āvarṇam*.

- The *mantra* of this *Āvarṇam* is the *Pancadaśī mantra* itself.
- *Sarva Kāma Siddhi Mudrā* and *Sarva Trikaṇḍā Mudrā* are controlling this *Āvarṇam*.
- Its *bīja* letter is '*Hrīm*'.
- The name of the *Chitśakti* in this *Chakra* is "*Parā Parādhi Rahasya Yoginī*". Since this form is not reachable through eyes or even mind.

This is the limit or border of all the happiness and hence the apt name "*Sarvānandamaya Chakram*".
The bliss that can be obtained from the unison of *Śiva* and *Śakti* – i.e. the soul and the *Brahmam* is the form of *Parā Parādhi Rahasya Yoginī*.

The fourth (*turīya*) *vidyā* is the place where all *mantras*, all mindsets, all *pīṭas*, all *yogas* and all *Siddhis* merge. We have reached the dwelling place of *Śrī Devī*. The supremacist (*paramporul*), who was united (*Advaitam*) in the end, was suffering from loneliness. That has become again two due to illusion (*Dvaitam*). This illusion is the root cause of this world. This *Ambikai Śakti* having various different names and forms, only creates and protects this world

The holy *bindu* at the center of the *Śrī Chakra*, when *Parabrahmam* decided to create this world, split into two viz., *Prakāśam* and *Vimarśam*.

- *Prakāśam* is the *Siddha Brahmam* (white *bindu*). The letter relating to this is '*A*' – in the form of *Śiva*.
- *Vimarśam* is the is the *Chitśakti* (blood – red *bindu*). The letter relating to this is '*Aha*' – in the form of *Śakti*.
- '*Aham*' is both *Prakāśam* and *Vimarśam* merging form. Such a union is the form of Bliss – *Sarvānandamaya Chakram*.

The form originated from the merging of *Prakāśam* and *Vimarśam* is the *Parāśakti* – *Parā* haughtiness. *Prakāśam*, *Vimarśam* and the *Parā* haughtiness are the triangle called *Bindu*. *Maheśwari Śakti* is the name of the illusion that controls the whole world. The blood-bindu gives the name and form. This *Bindu* is called as *Mahāpīṭam* or *Ānanda Pīṭam*. The integrated form of all the 51 *Śakti Pīṭas* is this *Bindu*.

The worshipper of this *Āvarṇam* is freed from all the worldly bonds and merges with *Brahmam*.

The *Navāvarṇa* song of *Śrī Muthuswamy Dīkṣitar* pertaining to this *Āvarṇa* begins with *"Śrī Kamalāmbā Jayati Ambā Jayati Śrī Kamalāmbā Jayati Jagadambā"*.

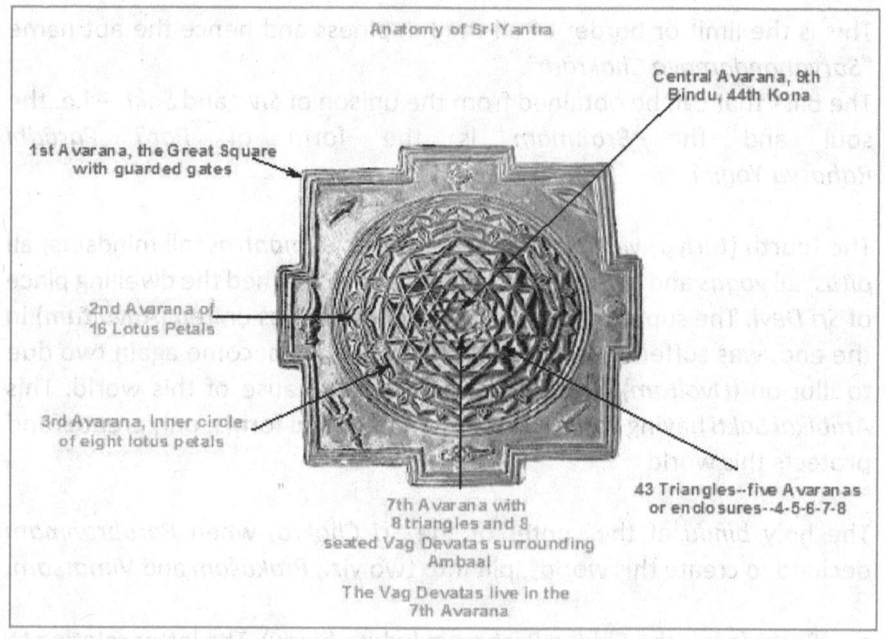

*****

Śrī Devī Khadgamāla Stotram
(Śrī Saharākṣarī Vidyā)

Śrī Devī Khadgamāla Stotram is in the middle of *Śrī Vāmakeśvara Tantra* as a dialogue between *Umādevī* and *Maheśvara*. *Sengālipuram Śrī Anantarāma Dīkṣatar* used to about *Śrī Devī Khadgamāla Stotram* - "if *Śrī Devī Khadgamāla Stotram* is chant, will not *Śrī Devī* come and stand before the chanter". Generally, this *mantra* is chant during *Śrī Chakra Navāvarṇa pooja*. This has 1000 letters in total and hence it is called as *Śrī Saharākṣarī Vidyā*. This has ~180 names. These names are used in *archanā* form also.

The names of all the above mentioned *Devīs* like *Siddhi Devīs*, *Aṣṭa Mātās*, *Gupta Yoginīs*, *Gupta Tara Yoginīs*, *Sampradāya Yoginīs*, *Kulotīrṇa Yoginīs*, *Nigarba Yoginīs* and all are revealed in *Śrī Devī Khadgamāla Stotram*. That is the splendor of it.

Just by chanting *Śrī Devī Khadgamāla Stotram*, one can get the fruits of complete *Navāvarṇa pooja*. It is said that, the ancestors get the satisfaction resulting from worshipping them in the prescribed manner, in crores of births, by simply chanting the *Śrī Devī Khadgamāla Stotram*. What a magnificence!

The verse is given below as to be used for chanting. The connection of the verses with *Navāvarṇa* is detailed in the next chapter.

Nyāsa:

Asya Śrī Śuddhaśakti Sambudyanta Mālā Mahāmantrasya |
Upastīndrayādiṣṭāyī Varuṇāditya Riṣaya: |
Devī Gāyatrī Canda: | *Sātvika Kakāra Baṭṭāraka Pīṭastita Śiva Kāmeśvarāṅka Nilayā Mahā Kāmeśvarī Śrī Lalitā Baṭṭārikā Devatā* ||
Om Aim Bījam | *Om Sou: Śakti:* | *Om Klīm Kīlakam* |
Mama Khadga Sidyarte Jape Viniyoga: ||

Aim Aṅguṣṭābhyām Nama: | *Klīm Darjanībhyām Nama:* |
Sou: Madhyamābhyām Nama: | *Aim Anāmikābhyām Nama:* |
Klīm Kanīṣṭikābhyām Nama: | *Sou: Karatala Karapruṣṭābhyām Nama:* |

Aim Hrudayāya Nama: | *Klīm Śiraśe Svāhā:* |
Sou: Śikāyai Vaśat | *Aim Kavacāya Gum* |
Klīm Netratrayāya Vouşaţ | *Sou: Astrāya Phaţ* |
Bhūrbhuvasuvaromiti Digbanda: ||

Dhyānam

Tādruśam Khadgamāpnoti *Ena Hastastitena Vai* |
Aşţādaśamahā Dvīpasamrāţ Bhoktā Bhavişyati ||

Lam Ityādji Pañca Pooja

Lam Pritviyātmikāyai Śrī Lalitāmbikāyai Gaṇḍam Samarpayāmi |
Ham Ākāśātmikāyai Śrī Lalitāmbikāyai Puşpai: Pūjayāmi |
Yam Vaivātmikāyai Śrī Lalitāmbikāyai Dhūpamāgrāyāmi |
Ram Vahniyātmikāyai Śrī Lalitāmbikāyai Dhīpam Darśayāmi |
Vam Amrutātmikāyai Śrī Lalitāmbikāyai Amrutam Mahāneivedhyam
                                      Nivedayāmi |
Sam Sarvātmikāyai Śrī Lalitāmbikāyai Sarvopacāra Pūjām Samarpayāmi

Om Aim Hrīm Śrīm Aim Klīm Sou:

Om Namas Tripurasundari, Hrudaya Devi, Śiro Devi, Śikā Devi, Kavaca Devi, Netra Devi, Astra Devi, Kāmeśvari, Baga Mālini, Nityaklinne, Beruṇḍe, Vahnivāsini, Mahāvajreśvari, Śivadhūti, Tvarite, Kulasundari, Nitye, Nīlapatāke, Vijaye, Sarvamaṅgaļe, Jvālāmālini, Citre, Mahānitye, Parameśvara-Parameśvari, Mitreśamayi, Şaşţīśamayi, Oḍyāṇamayi, Caryā Nādamayi, Lopāmurāmayi, Agastyamayi, Kālātāpanamayi, Dharmācāryamayi, Muktakeśīśvaramayi, Dīpakalānātamayi, Vişṇudevamayi, Prabhākaradevamayi, Tejodevamayi, Manojadevamayi,

Aṇimā Siddhe, Laghimā Siddhe, Mahimā Siddhe, Īşitva Siddhe, Vaşitva Siddhe, Prākāmya Siddhe, Buddhi Siddhe, Icchā Siddhe, Prāpti Siddhe, Mokśa Siddhe, Brahma Śakte, Śveta Varṇe, Śikhi Vāhanā, Śyāma Varṇā, Śyāmaļā, Śyāma Varṇā, Krişṇa Varṇā, Pīta Varṇā, Brāhmi, Māheśwari, Koumāri, Vaişṇavi, Vārāhi, Māhendri, Cāmuṇḍe, Mahālakśmi,

Sarva Samkśobiṇi, Sarva Vidrāviṇi, Sarvākarşiṇi, Sarva Vaśaṅkari, Sarvonmādini, Sarvamahāṅkuśe, Sarva Keśari, Sarva Bīje, Sarva Yone,

Sarva Trikaṇḍe, Prakaṭa Yogini, Bouddha Darśanāṅgi, Trailokya Mohana Chakrasvāmini,

Kāmākarṣiṇi, Buddhi Ākarṣiṇi, Ahaṅkārākarṣiṇi, Śabdākarṣiṇi, Sparśākarṣiṇi, Rūpākarṣiṇi, Rasākarṣiṇi, Gandākarṣiṇi, Siddhākarṣiṇi, Dairyākarṣiṇi, Smrutyākarṣiṇi, Nāmākarṣiṇi, Bījākarṣiṇi, Ātmākarṣiṇi, Amrutākarṣiṇi, Śarīrākarṣiṇi, Gupta Yogini, Sarvāvāśā Paripūraka Chakra Svāmini,

Ananga Kusume, Ananga Mekale, Ananga Madane, Ananga Madanā Ture, Ananga Rekhe, Ananga Veginī, Anangānguśe, Ananga Malini, Gupta Tara Yogini, Sarva Saṅkśobaṇa Chakra Svāminī, Pūrvāmnāya Digdevate, Sruṣṭirūpe,

Sarva Saṅkśobiṇi, Sarva Vidrāviṇi, Sarvākarṣiṇi, Sarvāhlādini, Sarva Sammohini, Sarva Stambini, Sarva Jrumbiṇi, Sarva Vaśaṅkari, Sarva Ranjani, Sarvonmādini, Sarvārthasādini, Sarva Sampatthi Pūrani, Sarva Mantramayī, Sarva Dvandva Kśayaṅkari, Sampradāya Yogini, Sarva Darṣanāṅgi, Sarva Sowbhāgya Dāyaka Chakra Svāminī,

Sarva Siddhi Pradhe, Sarva Sampath Pradhe, Sarva Priaṅkari, Sarva Maṅgala Kāriṇi, Sarva Kāma Pradhe, Sarva Dukkha Vimośani, Sarva Mrutyu Praśamani, Sarva Vigna Nivāriṇi, Sarvāṅga Sundari, Sarva Soubhāgya Dāyini, Kulottīrṇa Yogini, Sarvārta Sādaka Chakra Svāminī,

Sarva Jnānamayi, Sarvajne, Sarva Śakte, Sarvaiśvarya Pradhe, Sarva Gnānamayi, Sarva Vyādhi Nivāriṇī, Sarvādhāra Swarūpe, Sarva Pāpahare, Sarvānandamayī, Sarva Rakśā Swarūpiṇī, Sarvepsita Phalaprade, Nigarba Yogini, Vaiṣṇava Darśanāṅgi, Sarva Rakśākara Chakra Svāminī,

Vaśini, Kāmeśi, Modini, Vimale, Aruṇe, Jayinī, Sarveśvari, Koulini, Rahasya Yogini, Śākta Darśanāṅgi, Sarva Rogahara Chakra Svāminī, Paścimāmnāyeśi,

Danur Bāṇa Pāśāṅkuśa Devate, Kāmeśi, Vajreśi, Bagamālini, Atirahasya Yogini, Śaiva Darṣanāṅgi, Sarva Siddhiprada Chakra Svāminī, Uttarāmnāyeśi,

Samhārarūpe, Śuddhapare, Bindu Pīṭagate, Mahātripura Sundari, Parāparāti Rahasya Yoginī, Śambava Darśanāṅgi, Sarvānandamaya Chakra Svāminī,

Tripure, Tripureśī, Tripura Sundarī, Tripura Vāsinī, Tripurāśrī:, Tripura Mālinī, Tripura Siddhe, Tripurāmbā, Mahā Tripura Sundarī, Sarva Chakraste, Anuttarāmnāyākya Svarūpe, Mahā Tripura Bhairavī, Caturvida Guṇarūpe, Kule, Akule[28], Kulākule, Mahā Koulini, Sarvottare, Sarva Darśanāṅgi, Navāsana Stite, Navākśari, Nava Mitunakrute, Maheśa Mādava Vidātru Manmata Skanda Nandi Indra Manu Candra Gupera Agastrya Krodha Baṭṭārika Vidyātmike, Kalyāṇa Tatvatraya Rūpe, Śiva Śivātmike, Pūrṇa Brahma Śakte, Mahā Tripura Sundarī, Tava Pādukām Pūjayāmi Tarpayāmi Nama:

Śrīm Hrīm Aim Om (Svāhā) ||

Iti Śrī Vāmakeśvara Tantre Umāmaheśvara Samvāde
Devī Khadga Mālā Stotraratnam Samāptam

*****

---

[28] 96th name in Śrī Lalitā Sahasranāma – Akulā – अकुला

Navāvarṇa vs Khadgamāla Stotram

Let us now try to understand the connection between *Śrī Devī Khadga Māla Stotram* and the *Navāvarṇa pooja.*

<u>First *Āvarṇam;*</u> *Om Aim Hrīm Śrīm Aim Klīm Sou:*

Om Namas Tripurasundari, Hrudaya Devi, Śiro Devi, Śikā Devi, Kavaca Devi, Netra Devi, Astra Devi, Kāmeśvari, Baga Mālini, Nityaklinne, Beruṇḍe, Vahnivāsini, Mahāvajreśvari, Śivadhūti, Tvarite, Kulasundari, Nitye, Nīlapatāke, Vijaye, Sarvamaṅgaḷe, Jvālāmālini, Citre, Mahānitye, Parameśvara-Parameśvari, Mitreśamayi, Ṣaṣṭīśamayi, Oḍyāṇamayi, Caryā Nādamayi, Lopāmurāmayi, Agastyamayi, Kālātāpanamayi, Dharmācāryamayi, Muktakeśīśvaramayi, Dīpakalānātamayi, Viṣṇudevamayi, Prabhākaradevamayi, Tejodevamayi, Manojadevamayi,

First *Āvarṇam* – First line;

1. *Aṇimā Siddhe,*
2. *Laghimā Siddhe,*
3. *Mahimā Siddhe,*
4. *Īṣitva Siddhe,*
5. *Vaṣitva Siddhe,*
6. *Prākāmya Siddhe,*
7. *Buddhi Siddhe,*
8. *Icchā Siddhe,*
9. *Prāpti Siddhe,*
10. *Mokśa Siddhe,*

First *Āvarṇam* – Second line;

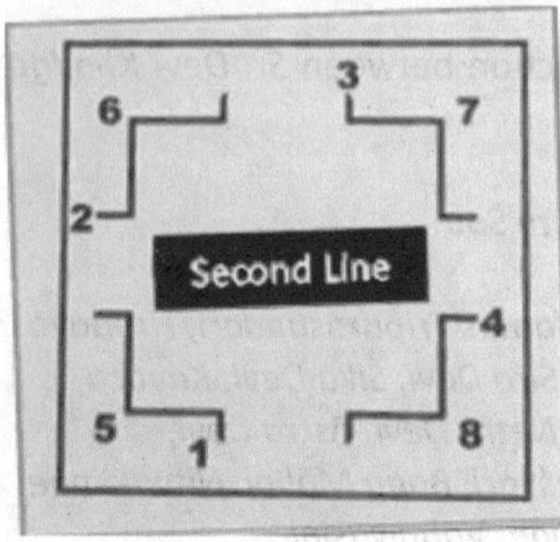

1. *Brahma Śakte – Brāhmi,*
2. *Śveta Varṇe – Māheśwari,*
3. *Śikhi Vāhanā – Koumāri,*
4. *Śyāma Varṇā – Vaiṣṇavi,*
5. *Śyāmaḷā – Vārāhi,*
6. *Śyāma Varṇā – Māhendri,*
7. *Kriṣṇa Varṇā – Cāmuṇḍā,*
8. *Pīta Varṇā – Mahālakśmi,*

First *Āvarṇam* – Third line;

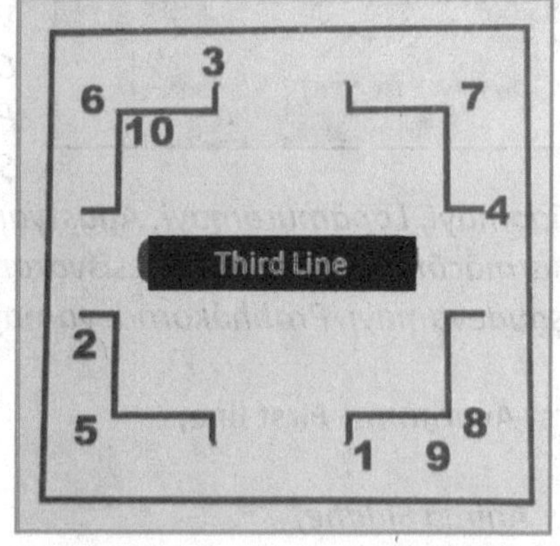

1. *Sarva Samkśobiṇi,*
2. *Sarva Vidrāviṇi,*
3. *Sarvākarṣiṇi,*
4. *Sarva Vaśaṅkari,*
5. *Sarvonmādini,*
6. *Sarvamahāṅkuśe,*
7. *Sarva Keśari,*
8. *Sarva Bīje,*
9. *Sarva Yone,*
10. *Sarva Trikaṇḍe,*

Prakaṭa Yogini, Bouddha Darśanāṅgi, Trailokya Mohana Chakrasvāmini,

Second *Āvarṇam*;

1. *Kāmākarṣiṇi,*
2. *Buddhi Ākarṣiṇi,*
3. *Ahaṅkārākarṣiṇi,*
4. *Śabdākarṣiṇi,*
5. *Sparśākarṣiṇi,*
6. *Rūpākarṣiṇi,*
7. *Rasākarṣiṇi,*
8. *Gandākarṣiṇi,*
9. *Siddhākarṣiṇi,*
10. *Dairyākarṣiṇi,*
11. *Smrutyākarṣiṇi,*
12. *Nāmākarṣiṇi,*
13. *Bījākarṣiṇi,*
14. *Ātmākarṣiṇi,*
15. *Amrutākarṣiṇi,*
16. *Śarīrākarṣiṇi,*

Gupta Yogini, Sarvāvāśā Paripūraka Chakra Svāmini,

Third *Āvarṇam*;

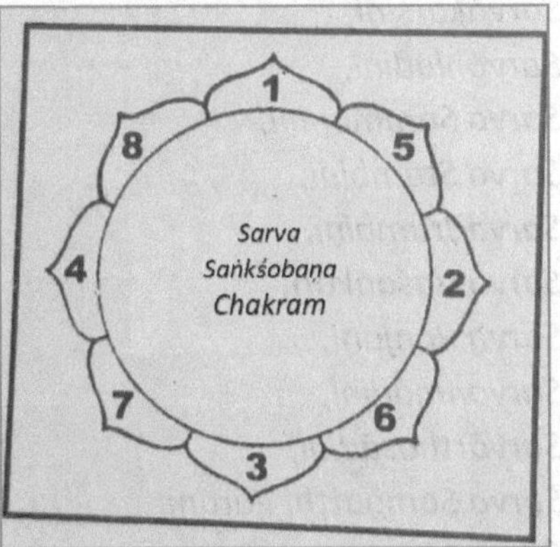

1. *Ananga Kusume,*
2. *Ananga Mekale,*
3. *Ananga Madane,*
4. *Ahaṅga Madanā Ture,*
5. *Ananga Rekhe,*
6. *Ananga Veginī,*

7. *Anangānguśe,*

8. *Ananga Malini,*

Gupta Tara Yogini, Sarva Saṅkśobaṇa Chakra Svāminī, Pūrvāmnāya
Digdevate, *Sruṣṭirūpe,*

<u>Fourth Āvarṇam</u>;

1. *Sarva Saṅkśobiṇi,*

2. *Sarva Vidrāviṇi,*

3. *Sarvākarṣiṇi,*

4. *Sarvāhlādini,*

5. *Sarva Sammohini,*

6. *Sarva Stambini,*

7. *Sarva Jrumbiṇi,*

8. *Sarva Vaśaṅkari,*

9. *Sarva Ranjani,*

10. *Sarvonmādini,*

11. *Sarvārthasādini,*

12. *Sarva Sampatthi Pūrani,*

13. *Sarva Mantramayī,*

14. *Sarva Dvandva Kśayaṅkari,*

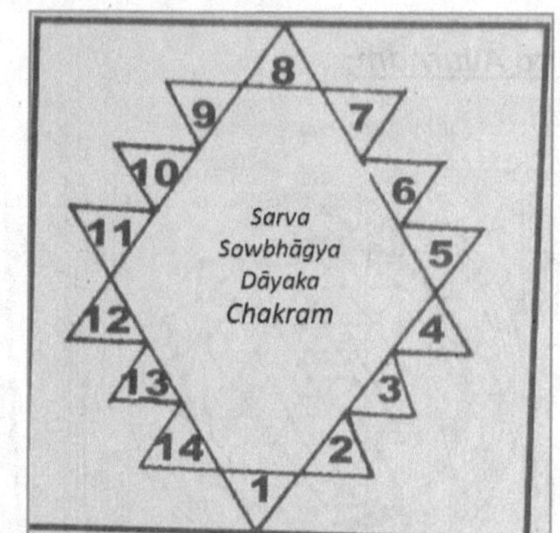

Sampradāya Yogini, Sarva Darṣanāṅgi, Sarva Sowbhāgya Dāyaka
Chakra Svāminī,

<u>Fifth Āvarṇam</u>;

1. Sarva Siddhi Pradhe,
2. Sarva Sampath Pradhe,
3. Sarva Priaṅkari,
4. Sarva Maṅgala Kāriṇi,
5. Sarva Kāma Pradhe,
6. Sarva Dukkha Vimośani,
7. Sarva Mrutyu Praśamani,
8. Sarva Vigna Nivāriṇi,
9. Sarvāṅga Sundari,
10. Sarva Soubhāgya Dāyini,

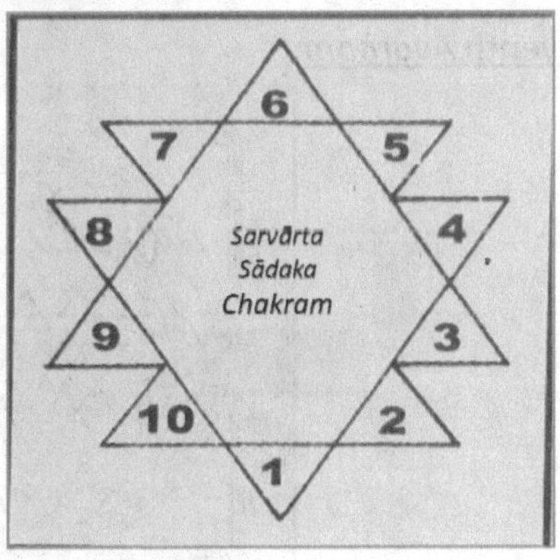

Kulottīrṇa Yogini, Sarvārta Sādaka Chakra Svāminī,

<u>Sixth Āvarṇam</u>;

1. *Sarvajne,*
2. *Sarva Śakte,*
3. *Sarvaiśvarya Pradhe,*
4. *Sarva Gnānamayi,*
5. *Sarva Vyādhi Nivāriṇī,*
6. *Sarvādhāra Swarūpe,*
7. *Sarva Pāpahare,*
8. *Sarvānandamayī,*
9. *Sarva Rakśā Swrūpiṇī,*
10. *Sarvepsita Phalaprade,*

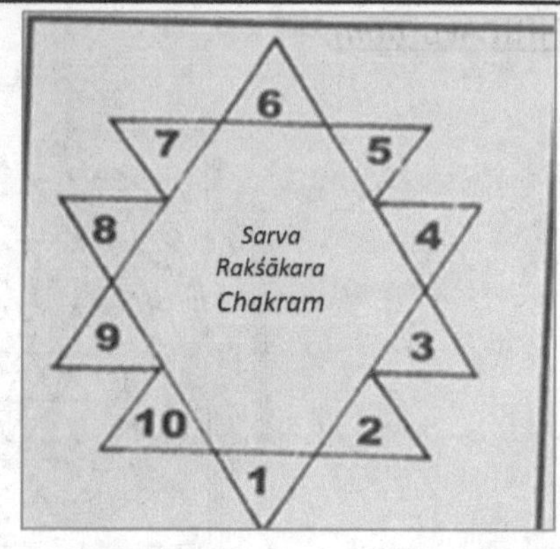

Nigarba Yogine, Vaiṣṇava Darśanāṅgi, Sarva Rakśākara Chakra Svāminī,

Seventh *Āvarṇam*;

1. *Vaśini,*
2. *Kāmeshi,*
3. *Modini,*
4. *Vimale,*
5. *Aruṇe,*
6. *Jayinī,*
7. *Sarveśvari,*
8. *Koulini,*

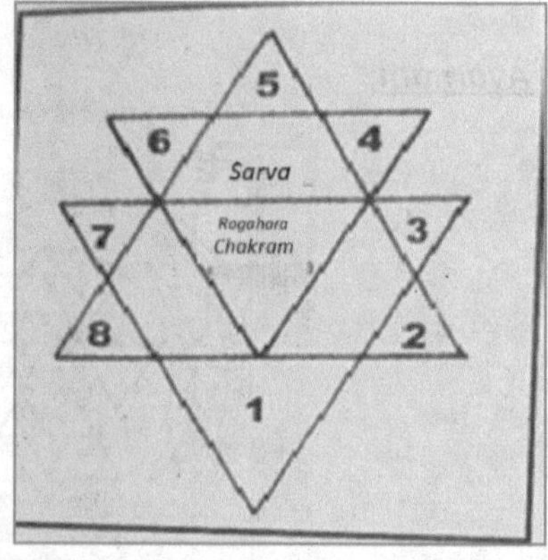

Rahasya Yogini, Śākta Darśanāṅgi, Sarva Rogahara Chakra Svāminī, Paścimāmnāyeśi,

Eighth *Āvarṇam*;

1. *Mahābāṇi*
2. *Puṣpacāpi*
3. *Puṣpapāśi*
4. *Anguśi*

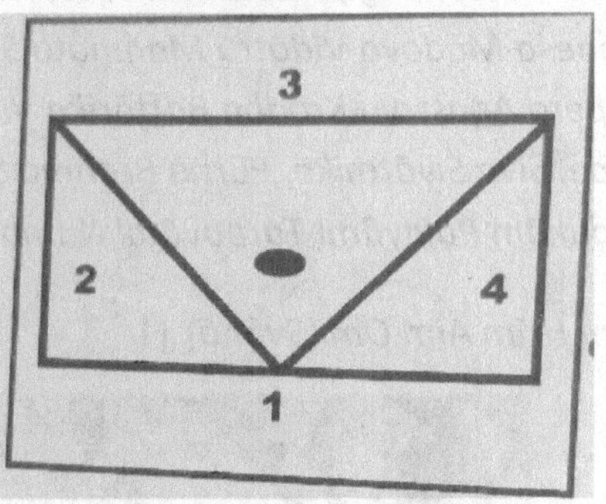

Danur Bāṇa Pāśāṅkuśa Devate, Kāmeśi, Vajreśi, Bagamālini, Atirahasya Yogini, Śaiva Darśanāṅgi, Sarva Siddhiprada Chakra Svāminī, Uttarāmnāyeśi,

Ninth *Āvarṇam*;

1. *Tripure,*
2. *Tripureśī,*
3. *Tripura Sundarī,*

4.　*Tripura Vāsinī,*
5.　*Tripurāśrī:,*
6.　*Tripura Mālinī,*
7.　*Tripura Siddhe,*
8.　*Tripurāmbā,*
9.　*Mahā Tripura Sundarī,*

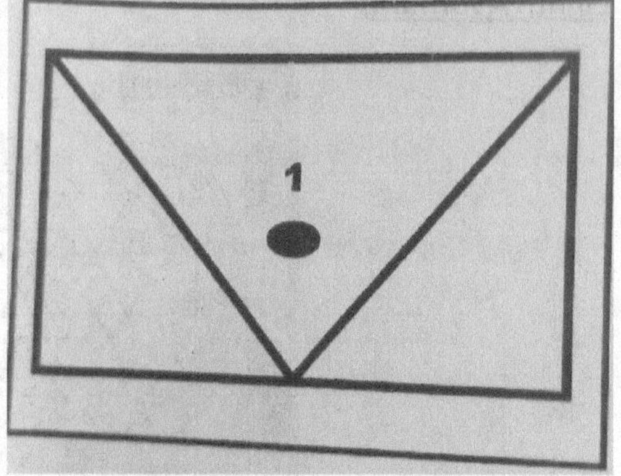

Sarva Chakraste,

Anuttarāmnāyākya Svarūpe,

Mahā Tripura Bhairavī,

Caturvida Guṇarūpe, Kule, Akule, Kulākule, Mahā Koulini, Sarvottare, Sarva Darśanāṅgi, Navāsana Stite, Navākśari, Nava Mitunakrute, Maheśa Mādava Vidātru Manmata Skanda Nandi Indra Manu Candra Gupera Agastrya Krodha Baṭṭārika Vidyātmike, Kalyāṇa Tatvatraya Rūpe, Śiva Śivātmike, Pūrṇa Brahma Śakte, Mahā Tripura Sundarī, Tava Pādukām Pūjayāmi Tarpayāmi Nama:

Śrīm Hrīm Aim Om (Svāhā) ||

*****

Seven Mothers

People worship *Śrī Devī* in various forms like, Seven Mothers (*Sapta Mātās*), *Sapta Kannikās*, *Nava Durgā*[29], *Dasha Mahā Vidyā*[30] and so on. In villages *Sapta Mātās* are used to be called as *Kannimār*. They are also called as *Kātthāyi, Karumāri, Mahamayi* and so on. Most of the *Devī* temples and even some *Śiva* temples have the idols of *Sapta Mātās*. Various texts like *Devī Bhāgavatam, Devī Purāṇam, Mārkaṇḍeya Purāṇam, Vāmana Purāṇam, Viṣṇu Dharmottaram, Mahākāli Māhātmyam* and so on so forth, describe about *Sapta Mātās*.

In the *Mahābhāratam* Lord *Kriṣṇa* went as a messenger of *Pāṇḍavās* to the palace of *Drudarāṣtran*. At that time, he showed his *Viṣvarūpam*. It is hailed that people could see the forms of *Sapta Mātās* in the *Viṣvarūpa* body of Lord *Kriṣṇa*.

The names of *Sapta Mātās* are – *Brāhmī, Maheśvarī, Koumārī, Vaiṣṇavī, Vārāhī, Aindrī* and *Cāmuṇḍī*. The story of their incarnations has been mentioned differently in various scripts.

Just before the killing of the demon *Antakāsura*, Lord *Śiva* was in *Yoga nidra*. *Antakāsura* tried to attack *Pārvati*. Immediately *Pārvati* thought of *Brahmā, Viṣṇu* and other *devas*. When *Pārvati*, as a lady was alone, devas did not want to help her in the male form and hence they took the female forms as;

1. The *Śakti* of *Brahmā* as *Brāhmī*,
2. The *Śakti* of *Maheṣvaran* as *Maheśvarī*,
3. The *Śakti* of *Kumaran* as *Koumārī*,
4. The *Śakti* of *Viṣṇu* as *Vaiṣṇavī*,
5. The *Śakti* of *Anantan* as *Vārāhī*. In some schools, it is also mentioned as the *Śakti* of the Goddess Earth.
6. The *Śakti* of *Indran* as *Aindrī*
7. The *Śakti* of *Eṣānar* as *Cāmuṇḍī*.

Lots of sub-*Śakti*s to the above *Devīs* also were formed from different *Devas*. *Pārvati Devī* ordered all these *Devīs* to fight with *Antakāsura*.

---

[29] *Śrī Devī Kavacam* details about *Nava Durgā*.
[30] This author has penned a separate book on *Dasha Mahā Vidyā* in English

When they were fighting, Lord *Śiva* waked up from *Yoga nidra* and stabbed *Antakāsura* with his trident. He sought the apology of Lord *Śiva* and *Pārvati Devī* while hanging from the trident. Lord *Śiva*, called as *Āśutoṣi*[31] forgave and made him the head of one of the *Gaṇas*. This incident has happened in *Tirukoilur* and that has been mentioned in that *Stala Purāṇam*.

Another story is mentioned in *Mārkaṇḍeya Purāṇam* – To assassinate *Mahiṣāsura*, *Śrī Devī* took the form of *Durgā*, as an integrated *Śakti* of all the *Devas* like *Brahmā*, *Viṣṇu*, *Indra* and various other *Devas*. Demons *Caṇḍa* and *Muṇḍa* frowned at the beauty of *Śrī Devī* wanted to marry **her**. They sent a messenger called *Sugrīvan*. This story is mentioned in *Śrī Devī Māhātmyam*. *Śrī Devī* with anger created various forms from different organs of her body like;

1. *Brāhmī* from face
2. *Maheśvarī* from naval
3. *Koumārī* from neck
4. *Vaiṣṇavī* from hands
5. *Vārāhī* from back
6. *Aindrī* from breasts
7. *Cāmuṇḍī* from forehead.

With the help of these *Devīs*, *Śrī Sarasvati Devi*, destroyed the demons *Caṇḍa* and *Muṇḍa*. These seven mothers got the boon of remaining at the first *Āvaraṇam* of *Śrī Chakram* called as *Trailokya Mohana Chakram*. They serve *Śrī Lalitā Devī* from here and bless the worshippers. Let us try to learn something about all these *Devīs* individually;

<u>**1.**</u> <u>***Brāhmī***</u>;

Among the three Gods (*Trimūrtis*), *Brahmā* is the first one. His task precedes others'. After he creating the creatures other two Gods can protect and destroy. In the same way *Brāhmī* is the first Goddess among the seven. He is the feature of *Brahmā*. Her vehicle is swan. She protects

---

[31] The meaning of *Āśutoṣi* is – giver of anything sought for.

everything in the west direction. She wears the skin of spotted deer as her dress. Worshipping *Brahmā* is related to worshipping Sun. Hence, it is told as, *Sandyā Devī* herself is in this form. She spreads the Sun rays, has four heads like *Brahmā*, has *Kamaṇḍalu*, Rosary, Books, etc., in her hand. While fighting she display herself with weapons in hand. This *Devi's*;

- *Bījā* (root) *mantra* – 'Brām'
- *Mantra* – *Om Brām Brāhmyai Nama:*
- *Gāyatrī* – *Om Brahma Śaktyai Ca Vidmahe Pītavarṇayai Ca Dīmahe Tanno Brāhmī Pracodayāt.*

2. <u>*Maheśvarī*</u>;

She blesses us sitting on a bull as a feature of Lord *Śivā* called as *Maheśvaran*. She has a Deer, an axe, a knife, a skull, safe and boon signet hands and five faces. She has an eye on the forehead and a crescent on the head. With all these she protects all of us. She is amidst and feel happy among the sages and *Veda* chanting of groups of *Nandis*.

Demon *Mahiśāsura* was killed by her trident only. '*Maha*' means *yagna*. Only when the *yagnas* are properly and abundantly performed rain will not fail and the country will prospect. She is the protector of such *yagnas*.

This *Devi's*;

- Colour is white
- *Bījā* (root) *mantra* – 'Mām'
- *Mantra* – *Om Mām Māheśvaryai Nama:*
- *Gāyatrī* – *Om Śveta Varṇāyai Ca Vidmahe Śūla Hastāyai Ca Dīmahe Tanno Maheśvarī Pracodayāt.*

3. <u>Koumārī</u>;

Koumārī is the feature of *Kumāran*, son of Lord *Śiva*. Her vehicle is peacock. She has other names like *Şaşţi Devi*, *Devasenā* and so on. She has six heads; twelve hands and she hold a divine spear and leads the army. She originated from the neck of *Śrī Devī*. She bestows children.

This *Devi's*;

* Colour is red
* *Bījā* (root) *mantra – 'Goum'*
* *Mantra – Om Goum Koumāryai Nama*:
* *Gāyatrī – Om Śikhi Vāhanāyai Ca Vidmahe Śakti Hastāyai Ca Dīmahe Tanno Koumārī Pracodayāt.*

4. <u>Vaiṣnavī</u>;

Vaiṣṇavī is a feature of *Mahāviṣṇu* and originated from the hands of *Parāśakti*. Religions texts do indicate that male form of *Parāśakti* is *Viṣṇu*. In most of the places it has been mentioned that *Viṣṇu's* sister is *Parāśakti*. In the form of *Śaṅkara Nārāyaṇa*, the left half of *Śiva* is *Viṣṇu*. In the form of *Arddhanārīśvara*[32], the left half of *Śiva* is *Parāśakti*. What does this indicate? *Viṣṇu* and *Parāśakti* are one and the same. The sentence, "*Bhokeca Bhavāni, Puruṣeca Viṣṇu, Krodeca Kāli, Samareca Durgā*" is worth comparable in this context. The protecting Goddess *Mahālakśmi*, in the form of *Vaiṣṇavī* sits on an Eagle (*Garuda*), with a peaceful face, with conch and chakra in the hands, bestows all wealth, health and all to her devotees.

---

[32] 392nd name in *Śrī Lalitā Sahasranāma – Śrīkanṭhārdhaśarīriṇī* - श्रीकण्ठार्धशरीरिणी

This *Devi's*;

- Colour is white
- *Bījā* (root) *mantra – 'Vaim'*
- *Mantra – Om Vaim Vaiṣṇavyai Nama*:
- *Gāyatrī – Om Śyāma Varṇāyai Ca Vidmahe Chakra Hastāyai Ca Dīmahe Tanno Vaiṣṇavī Pracodayāt.*

5. *Vārāhī*;

Vārāhī originated from the back portion of *Parāśakti* and is a feature of *Anantan*. Some schools opine that she is a feature of the Goddess Earth and some say that she is a feature Vārāha incarnation of lord *Viṣṇu*. In a way these two are connected, since during *Vārāha* incarnation, lord *Viṣṇu* married Goddess Earth. She has a face of a boar. She is the knight of the army of *Parāśakti*. She is called by other names like *Pañcami*, *Daṇḍini*, *Daṇḍanāthā* and so on.

During the battle with *Tārukāsuran*, she was the chief of army for *Kāli*. During the battle with *Sumbāsuran*, she was the chief of army for *Caṇḍī Devī*. During the battle with *Baṇḍāsuran*, she was the chief of army for *Śrī Lalitā Devī*. Her chariot is called *Giri Chakram*. She has a hull in her hand. The statement *"Vārāhī Vīrya Nandanā"* means – she is full of velour, fire and anger. There used to be a saying that "don't argue with the devotee of *Vārāhī*. She has various vehicles like Lion, Deer, Snake, etc. The nine days during month of *Ādi* (July-August) is celebrated as *"Vārāhi Navarāthri"*.

This *Devi's*;

- Colour is black
- *Bījā* (root) *mantra – 'Vām'*
- *Mantra – Om Vām Vārāhyai Nama*:
- *Gāyatrī – Om Śyāmalāyai Ca Vidmahe Hala Hastāyai Ca Dīmahe Tanno Vārāhī Pracodayāt.*

6. *Aindrī*;

Only if a person has performed 1000 *Aśvameda yagnas*, he is eligible to become the post of *Indran*. He is the head of 300 crores of *Devas* and *Aṣṭa Dik Bālās*. *Aindrī* is a feature of such an Indran and originated from the breast portion of *Parāśakti*. Hence, she has that *Irāvata* elephant itself as her vehicle. She has *Kulicam* and Thunder Bolt (*Vajrāyutam*) in her hands. She bestows beauty, courage and rich life to her devotees. She is indicated as *Indrāṇi*.

This *Devi's*;

- Colour is Indra Blue stone. In some places it is also mentioned as white.
- *Bījā* (root) *mantra – 'Īm'*
- *Mantra – Om Īm Aindriyai Nama*:
- *Gāyatrī – Om Śyāma Varṇāyai Ca Vidmahe Vajra Hastāyai Ca Dīmahe Tanno Aindrī Pracodayāt.*

7. *Cāmuṇḍī*;

Cāmuṇḍī originated from the forehead of *Parāśakti* and is a feature of *Īśānan*. According to *Śrī Devī Mahātmiyam*, she destroyed the demons like *Caṇḍan* and *Muṇḍan* and hence this name. In the state Karnataka, *Śrī Devī* is worshipped in the name of *Cāmuṇḍī*. In Mysore there is a world-famous temple for *Cāmuṇḍī*. In various villages there are deities called *Cāmuṇḍī*. She has a corpse as her vehicle. She is red in colour and courageous and hence bestows success to her devotees.

This *Devi's*;

- Colour is black. In some places it has been mentioned as Red.

- *Bījā* (root) *mantra* – '*Cām*'
- *Mantra* – *Om Cām Cāmuṇḍāyai Nama*:
- *Gāyatrī* – *Om Kriśṇa Varṇāyai Ca Vidmahe Śula Hastāyai Ca Dīmahe Tanno Cāmuṇḍī Pracodayāt.*

<u>*Sapta* Mothers – a summary</u>;

A demon called *Tārukan*, did deep penance with *Brahmā* and he got a boon of immortality. He also got the strength of *Amruta* and *Brahma Daṇḍam* and hence he was roaming with ego. He installed his kingdom in the world of *Devas* and harassed *Devas*. *Devas* prayed with *Brahmā* and he cursed *Tārukan* that he would be destroyed by a lady. All *Devas*, including *Brahmā*, *Viṣṇu*, *Rudra* and all prayed *Śrī Devī*. Seven Mothers originated from her as described earlier. *Maheśvari* stabbed *Tārukan* and from his blood, lot many demons originated. *Tārukan* trumpeted Lord *Śiva*. *Badra Kāli* originated from Lord *Śiva*'s third eye on the forehead. Her image was so scary that *Pārvati* herself was terrified. On *Pārvati*'s request *Badra Kāli* reduced to somewhat peaceful image with 3 eyes and 16 hands. She drank all the blood oozing from the body of *Tārukan* and killed him alongwith seven Mothers.

We have separate temples for seven Mothers in many a place. In some temples, there is separate shrines. Some worth noting are – Seven Mothers temple at Karuppur near Jeeyapuram at Trichy, Tamilnadu. There is a special shrine for seven Mothers in the Māngādu temple at Chennai in the west behind the main deity. There is another temple seven mothers at Vālāḍi village near Trichy.

Let us worship seven mothers and get all types of blessings.

Sapta Mothers – at a glance;

Mother	*Śakti*	Originated from (organ)	Colour	*Bījam*	*Mantram*	*Gāyatrī*
Brāhmī	Brahmā	Face		Brām	Om Brām Brāhmyai Nama	Om Brahma Śaktyai Ca Vidmahe Pītavarṇayai Ca Dīmahe Tanno Brāhmī Pracodayāt
Maheśvarī	Maheśvaran	Naval	White	Mām	Om Mām Māheśvaryai Nama	Om Śveta Varṇayai Ca Vidmahe Śūla Hastāyai Ca Dīmahe Tanno Maheśvarī Pracodayāt
Koumārī	Kumāran	Neck	Red	Goum	Om Goum Koumāryai Nama	Om Śikhi Vāhanāyai Ca Vidmahe Śakti Hastāyai Ca Dīmahe Tanno Koumārī Pracodayāt
Vaiṣṇavī	Viṣṇu	Hands	White	Vaim	Om Vaim Vaiṣṇavyai Nama	Om Śyāma Varṇāyai Ca Vidmahe Chakra Hastāyai Ca Dīmahe Tanno Vaiṣṇavī Pracodayāt
Vārāhī	Anantan or Goddess Earth	Back	Black	Vām	Om Vām Vārāhyai Nama	Om Śyāmalāyai Ca Vidmahe Hala Hastāyai Ca Dīmahe Tanno Vārāhī Pracodayāt
Aindrī	Indran	Breast	Indra Blue stone or white	Īm	Om Īm Aindriyai Nama	Om Śyāma Varṇāyai Ca Vidmahe Vajra Hastāyai Ca Dīmahe Tanno Aindrī Pracodayāt
Cāmuṇḍī	Īśānan	Forehead	Black/red	Cām	Om Cām Cāmuṇḍyai Nama	Om Kriśṇa Varṇāyai Ca Vidmahe Śūla Hastāyai Ca Dīmahe Tanno Cāmuṇḍī Pracodayāt

*****

Nityā Devīs

In the *Śrī Chakra*, around the *Bindu*, on each of the three sides of the triangle, 5 *Nityā Devis* are sitting – totally 15 *Nityā Devis*. They are immortal and identify the time. They are respectively – *Kameśvari, Bagamālini, Nityaklinnā, Beruṇḍā, Vahnivāsinī, Mahā Vajreśvari, Śivadhūti, Tvaritā, Kulasundarī, Nityā, Nīlapatākā, Vijayā, Sarvamaṅgalā, Jvālāmālinī* and *Chitrā*. At the center *Śrī Devī* herself decorate the *Bindu* as 16th *Mahā Nityā Devi*.

These 16 *Nityā Devis* alongwith *Śyāmalā* and *Vārāhi* stand protecting the *Śrī Chakra*.

Māta: Maho Tayite Lalite Hayāsya Kumbodbhavāti Sannuta Divya Kīrtte |
Kāmeśvari Prakruti Titi Devatāpi: Samsevitāṅgri Yugaḷe | |

The summary meaning of the above verse is – Enchanting beautiful, without leaving Lord *Śivā*, adored by scholars like *Hayagrīva, Agastya* and all, shining in the center of the *Śrī Chakra*, starting from the bottom of the triangle in the anti-clockwise worshipped as 15 *Titi Nityā Devis*, viz., *Kameśvari, Bagamālini* and so on. Our humble *pranāms* to her.

These 15 *Nityās* represent 15 *titis* and hence they are called as *Titi Nityās*. During bright lunar fortnight from *Pratama* till *Pourṇami* (full moon) – from *Kameśvari* to *Chitrā*. During dark lunar fortnight from *Pratama* till *Amāvāsya* (new moon) – from *Chitrā* to *Kameśvari*. 16th *Nityā Devī* is *Parāśakti* herself.

There are crescent moons optimally pertaining to each of the *Titi Nityā*
Devīs, because the facial region of
Śrī Lalitā Devī shines like a full
Moon 16 crescents integrated
within.

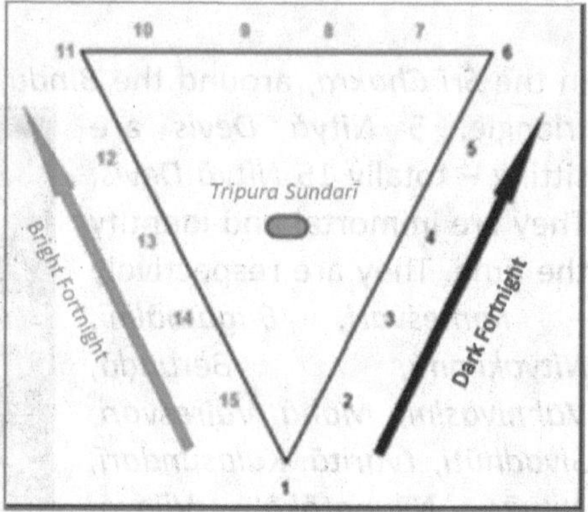

Each of the 15 letters of
Pañcadaśākṣarī mantra pertain
to each of the 15 *Titi Nityā Devīs*.
Hence *Pañcadaśākṣarī mantra*
and *Titi Nityās* are synonyms. All
causal of the soul is *Mahānityai*.

Each of the *Nityās* is in *Prakāśa*[33] form during day time and *Vimarśa* form
during night. They are also in the form of time and hence they are call
Kāla Atiṣṭāna Devīs.

#	Nityā Devī	Crescent Moon	Bright Lunar Fortnight	Dark Lunar Fortnight
1.	Kameśvari	Amrutakalā	Pratamai	New Moon
2.	Bagamālini	Mānatā	Dvitiyai	Caturdaśi
3.	Nityaklinnā	Pūṣā	Tritiyai	Trayodaśi
4.	Beruṇḍā	Tuṣṭi	Caturtti	Dvādaśi
5.	Vahnivāsinī	Puṣṭi	Pañcami	Ekādaśi
6.	Mahā Vajreśvari	Rati	Śaṣṭi	Daśami
7.	Śivadhūti	Truti	Saptami	Navami
8.	Tvaritā	Cacini	Aṣṭami	Aṣṭami
9.	Kulasundarī	Candrikā	Navami	Saptami
10.	Nityā	Śānti	Daśami	Śaṣṭi
11.	Nīlapatākā	Jyotsnā	Ekādaśi	Pañcami
12.	Vijayā	Śrīkalā	Dvādaśi	Caturtti
13.	Sarvamaṅgalā	Prīti	Trayodaśi	Tritiyai
14.	Jvālāmālinī	Angatā	Caturdaśi	Dvitiyai
15.	Chitrā	Pūrṇā	Full Moon	Pratamai
16.	Mahā Nityā	Pūrṇāmruta Sāgarā	Parāśakti, the paradise always shining with 16 crescents.	

---

[33] *Prakāśa* and *Vimarśa*, the Light of Consciousness and the Power of Self-Awareness respectively

It is evident from the names in *Śrī Lalitā Sahasranāma*, that *Śrī Lalitā Devī* herself is in the forms of each of the *Nityā Devīs*.

#	*Nityā Devī*	# in *Lalitā Sahasranāma*	Name in *Lalitā Sahasranāma*
1.	*Kameśvari*	33, 77, 82, 373	Various names
2.	*Bagamālini*	277	*Bagamālini*
3.	*Nityaklinnā*	388	*Nityaklinnā*
5.	*Vahnivāsinī*	352	*Vahni Maṇḍala Vāsinī*
6.	*Mahā Vajreśvari*	468	*Vajreśvari*
7.	*Śivadhūti*	405	*Śivadhūti*
10.	*Nityā*	136	*Nityā*
12.	*Vijayā*	346	*Vijayā*
13.	*Sarvamaṅgalā*	200	*Sarvamaṅgalā*
14.	*Jvālāmālinī*	71	*Jvālāmālinīkakśipta Vahni Prākāra Madyagā*

In the tradition of *Śrī Vidyā*, worshipping *Titi Nityā Devis* is an important part. We saw that *Śrī Devi* herself is in the form of all these *Nityā Devis*. She herself takes the role of 16th *Nityā Devi*, called *Mahā Nityā Devi*.

The text called "*Tantra Rāja Tantram*" describes about *Nityā Devis* in detail. It has been mentioned that *Titi Nityā Devis* are connected subtle sound originations. They are in the form of time alongwith 36 philosophies. They are the vowels in Samskruta language. They are the universe. One Year has 360 days and 360 nights (totaling 720). There are 720 aspects of *Devis* in a year. Each *Devi* rules 100 *Nāḍis* in our body. Our body has 72,000 *Nāḍis*. The full circle of the *Nityās* also represents the 21,600 breaths a human being takes in a full day and night.

Other *Śāstra* texts mention that they are integrated with the five base elements like ether, air, etc. They are the 15 letters of *Pañcadaśākśarī mantra*. They are the bright lunar fortnights, as the names given in Vedas – *Darśā, Druṣṭā*[34], etc.

---

[34] These names are listed elsewhere in this chapter

The book *Tantra Rāja Tantram*, explains pooja methods alongwith meditation verses and all, individually for each of these *Titi Nityā Devis*. The meditation verses and the images may vary depending on the wish and request of the worshipper. The philosophy that these *Titi Nityā Devis* and the *Śrī Chakram* are integrated, is *Meru Prastāram*.

It has been mentioned in various places in *Śrī Lalitā Sahasranāmam* about *Titi Nityā Devis*. *Śrī Bhāskararāyar*, in his *Bhāṣyam*, explains;

73rd name – *Nityāparākramāṭopa Nirīkṣaṇa Samutsukā* – नित्यापराक्रमाटोप निरीक्षण समुत्सुका;

Once in the course of the battle with *Bhaṇḍasura*, two of his generals *Damanaka* and *Chitragupta* surrounded the *Śrī Chakrarāja* chariot and started waging a war by unfair means; at that time the 15 *Titi Nityā Devis* proved their prowess by destroying them in front of *Śrī Devī*, much to **Her** delight. **She** was enthused by the *Nitya Devi*'s celebrating the invasion of the enemy's army.

Because of their permanence (immortality), the *Ātma Śaktis* (the soul) are called *Nityās*. *Parākramāṭopa* – growing due to inward self-realization. One who is pleased with that. A person attains external bliss when the immortal soul power wins over the demonic forces, which raise their head from time to time within the mind.

391st name – *Nityā Ṣoḍaśikārūpā* – नित्या षोडशिकारूपा;

We have presiding deities for the 15 days from first to full moon day. They are all the limbs of *Śrī Devī*. *Śrī Devī* herself is the sixteenth *Nityā* – i.e. *Mahānityā*. **She** is also called as *Sādākya Kalā*. The description, method of *pooja*, *mantra*, *yantra*, etc., are described in detail in *Tantra Rāja Tantra*.

The 15 titis and names accordingly *Śākta* and *Veda*[35] tradition are;

---

[35] These names can be observed during annual *Upākarma*, at the start of *Vedas*.

Śākta Veda Tradition	Bright lunar fortnight		Dark lunar fortnight	
	Days	**Nights**	**Days**	**Nights**
Kāmeśwarī	*Samgnānam*	*Darṣā*	*Prastutam*	*Sudhā*
Bagamālinī	*Vignanām*	*Druṣṭā*	*Viśtutam*	*Sunvatī*
Nityaklinnā	*Pragnānam*	*Darśatā*	*Samstutam*	*Prasūtā*
Beruṇḍā	*Jānat*	*Viśvarūpā*	*Kalyānam*	*Sūyamānā*
Vahnivāsinī	*Abhinānat*	*Sudarṣanā*	*Viṣvarūpā*	*Abhiśūyamānā*
Mahāvajreśwarī	*Sankalpamānam*	*Āpyāyamānām*	*Sūkram*	*Bhītī*
Śivadūtī	*Prakalpamānam*	*Pyāyamānām*	*Amrutam*	*Prabhā*
Twaritā	*Upakalpamānam*	*Āpyāyā*	*Teśavī*	*Śambā*
Kulasundarī	*Upakluptam*	*Sunrutā*	*Teha:*	*Trupti*
Nityā	*Kluptam*	*Irā*	*Samittam*	*Tarpayantī*
Nīlapatākā	*Sreya:*	*Āpūryamānā*	*Aruṇam*	*Kāntā*
Vijayā	*Vasīya:*	*Pūryamānā*	*Bānumat*	*Kāmyā*
Sarvamaṅgalā	*Āyat*	*Pūrāyantī*	*Marīchimat*	*Kāmajātā*
Jvālāmālinī	*Sambūtam*	*Pūrṇā*	*Abitapat*	*Āyushmatī*
Chitrā	*Būtam*	*Pourṇamāsī*	*Tapasvat*	*Kāmadukā*

We are aware that the, according to *Vedas*, bright lunar fortnight has been divided in three parts viz. 5, 6 and 4. This indicates the 3 *kūṭas* in the *Pañcadaśī mantra*.

These *Titi Nityās* are worshipped from *Kāmeshwarī* to *Chitra* during bright lunar fortnight and from *Chitra* to *Kāmeshwarī* during dark lunar fortnight.

These *Titi Nityās Devīs* indicate that *Śrī Devī* is in the form of era. *Bāvano Upaniṣad* advises as; "*Pancadaśa Titirūpeṇa Kālasya Pariṇāma Valokanam*.

During the bright lunar fortnight, the Moon grows by absorbing the rays of the Sun. During dark lunar fortnight the brightness of the Moon decreases step by step. The *Titi Nityās* are also in this form.

For further reading about *Titi Nityās*, the book *Tantra Rāja Tantram* and/ or the *Lakśmīdhara's* explanation for the 32nd verse of *Soundaryalaharī* can be referred.

610th name – *Pratipan Mukhyarākānta Titimaṇḍalapūjitā* –
प्रतिपन्मुख्याराकान्त तिथि मण्डल पूजिता;

Pratipat means *Pratama*, the first day. *Rākā* means full Moon. She is being worshipped in all these fifteen days. The *Veda* names given in the above table, for each of the fifteen days. Above all these there is a *kalā* called *Sādā* in the galaxy of Moon (*Candramaṇḍala*). All these sixteen are called *Titimaṇḍala*.

Titinityā Yajanam is an important part of *Śrī Vidyā* worship. It has been mentioned in *Varāha Purāṇa* that *Agni* (fire) and other gods are the presiding deities for all these *Tities*.

<u>775th name</u> – *Merunilayā* – मेरुनिलया;

According to the saying; *Meru*: *Sumeru*: *Hemādri*: – *Meru* is a golden mountain. It can be reminded that this was mentioned in the 55th name *Sumeru Madhya Sruñggastā*. It is said that *Śrī Devī's Chintāmaṇi* house is at the top of the center peak.

After the demolition of the demon *Bhaṇḍāsura*, *Devas* ordered their architect *Viśvakarma* and the architect of demons *Mayan*, to construct an appropriate place for *Kāmeśwarā* and *Kāmeśwarī*. It was the *Deva's* wish that in the ocean called *Nitya Gnānam* in the midst of 16 *kṣetrās*, *Śrī Devī* should dwell in 16 forms, in the 16 cities decorated with gems, for the protection of this universe.

Accordingly, those architects constructed 16 cities in the 16 *kṣetrās*. These are on the top of 9 mountains and 7 oceans. These 16 cities were named as *Kāmeśwarī*, *Bagamālāpurī*, etc., based on the names of *Titi Nityās*. Out of these there are three peaks to the East, South-west, South-east and center of *Meru* mountain. In those three peaks there are the residences of *Brahmā*, *Vishṇu* and *Śiva* and in the center the residence of *Śrī Devī*.

Śrī city is located above all the *Brahmāṇḍās*, in a peninsula of gems amidst the ocean of nectar. There is many a nursery like multi treed *Mahotdyānam*, *Mandāra Vāṭikā*, *Kalpa Vāṭikā*, *Santāna Vāṭikā*, *Harisanta Vāṭikā*, *Pārijāta Vāṭikā*, *Kadamba Vana Vāṭikā* and so on surrounding this city. Further this city is encircled by different forts made of Iron, Steel, Copper, Lead, Brass, Five Metals, Silver, Gold, Topaz, Sardius, Aromatic, Diamond, Chrysoprase, Indigo Blue, Pearl, Emerald, Coral, Nine Gems and various gems and metals. Also surrounded by different theories like mind, intellect and ego and further surrounded by luster of Sun, Moon and Cupid.

There lies the house of *Chintāmaṇi* in this city. Within this cited is the *Śrī Chakra*. In the center of this on the seat of Five *Brahmas*, on the great throne – on the *Bindu* plank called *Sarvānandamayam* – seated is the great *Mahā Tripura Sundarī* gracing us all.

Tantrarāja Tantra (28th chapter) describes such a construction of *Śrī* city. *Vidopākyānam* also has details. *Lalithopākyānam*, *Lalitāstavaratnam* and *Chintāmaṇi Stavam* may be referred for more details about *Śrī* city and *Chintāmaṇi* house.

Tantrarāja Tantra (28th chapter) explains that *Nityā Devīs* are in the form of the worlds and time and their interchange. Accordingly, *Śrī Devī* dwells in the *Mahā Meru* during the first year of *Kruta Yuga* (*Kruta* era). *Nityā Devīs* starting from *Kāmeśwarī* till *Jvālāmālinī* live in other *Jambu Dvīpam*, *Plakśa Dvīpam*, etc. and seven oceans. *Chitrā Nityā* lives in the outside ether. In the next years each *Nitya Devī* (including *Śrī Devī*) moves to the next place. In the same way in the following years they move to adjacent places. In the sixteenth year they return to their original places. Each of the *Nityā Devī*s becomes the Moon of *Meru* in one year. (Further details in this regard can be had from the original book and its commentary called *Manorama*).

<u>784th name</u> – *Prāṇarūpiṇī* – प्राणरूपिणी;

One breath is to once inhale and exhale. The calculation of time as day, month, etc., is done by breath only. *Titi Nityā Devīs* are in the form of time. Since the time origins from breath, it can be taken as that *Titi Nityā Devīs* are the breath. *Śrī Devī* is also one of the *Titi Nityā Devīs* and hence **She** is *Prāṇarūpiṇī*. The related verses in *Tantra Rāja Tantra* (27th chapter) may be referred; *Athaṣoḍasa Nityānām Kālena Prāṇatochyate*.

<u>22nd verse</u> in *Phalasruti* part of *Śrī Lalitā Sahasranāmam* – On the full

Moon day, one should meditate by imagining Śrī *Devī* on the Full Moon, after offering the five oblations and these thousand names should be read. The night of the full Moon day is the last night of bright fortnight of the Moon. This has to be chant in the night only when the full Moon *titi* spans at that time.

On the full Moon day, *Śrī Devī* has to be imagined on the full Moon. All the fifteen *Titi Nityā Devīs* and the 16th *kalā* called *Sādā* also shine in the form of full Moon. The evidence for this is the 240th name *Candramaṇḍalamadhyagā*.

Let us try to understand about each of *Titi Nityā Devīs* individually;

1. *Kāmeśwarī*;

She blesses us all holding Noose, sugarcane bow, wine vessel, goad, flower arrows and boon signet in hands, red in colour, three eyes[36] and with a crescent moon in the head.

This *Devi's Gāyatrī – Om Kāmeśwaryai Ca Vidmahe Nityakklinnāyai Ca Dīmahe Tanno Nityā Pracodayāt*.

By worshipping this *Devi*, the devotees get the results like – happiness, wealth, peace and liberation.

2. *Bagamālinī*;

She blesses us all holding in her six hands, Lotus, Red Rose, Noose, bow, goad and flower arrows, sitting on a lotus flower with a smile on her face.

This *Devi's Gāyatrī – Om Bagamālinyai Ca Vidmahe Sarva Vaśaṅkaryai Ca Dīmahe Tanno Nityā Pracodayāt*.

---

[36] 453rd name in *Śrī Lalitā Sahasranāmam* is *Trinayanā*

By worshipping this *Devi*, the devotees get the results like – attracting all, protection of the womb and success in all tasks.

3. *Nityaklinnā*;
She blesses us all holding in her 4 hands noose, goad, *Abhaya* (no fear) signet and drinking vessel. She is red in colour, has three eyes and sits in a lotus flower.

This *Devi's Gāyatrī* – *Om Nityaklinnāyai Ca Vidmahe Nitya Mantrāyai Ca Dīmahe Tanno Nityā Pracodayāt.*

By worshipping this *Devi*, the devotees get the results like – co-operation in the family and love and affection.

4. *Berunḍā*;

She blesses us all holding in her hands, lotus flower, garland for *japam*, *Abhaya* (no fear) signet and conch. She is white in colour, has a crescent in her head.

This *Devi's Gāyatrī* – *Om Beruṇḍāyai Ca Vidmahe Viṭiharāyai Ca Dīmahe Tanno Nityā Pracodayāt.*

By worshipping this *Devi*, the devotees get the results like – health body and satiation of all wises.

5. *Vahnivāsinī*;

She blesses us holding in her 8 hands – conch, chakra, sugarcane bow, lotus flower, a *kalasam* (pot), noose and goad. She has three eyes and She is in golden colour.

This *Devi's Gāyatrī* – *Om Vahnivāsinyai Ca Vidmahe Siddhipradāyai Ca Dīmahe Tanno Nityā Pracodayāt.*

By worshipping this *Devi*, the devotees get the results like – health body and satiation of all tasks/ wishes.

6. *Mahāvajreśwarī*;

She blesses us holding in her hands – pomegranate fruit, sugarcane bow, noose and goad. She has three eyes. She is also called as *Bhavāni Mātā*.

This *Devi's Gāyatrī – Om Mahāvajreśwarīyai Ca Vidmahe Vajranityāyai Ca Dīmahe Tanno Nityā Pracodayāt.*

By worshipping this *Devi*, the devotees get the results like – getting rid of all sorrows.

7. *Śivadūtī*;

She blesses us with 8 hands, shining like a Sun.

This *Devi's Gāyatrī – Om Śivadūtyai Ca Vidmahe Śivankaryai Ca Dīmahe Tanno Nityā Pracodayāt.*

By worshipping this *Devi*, the devotees get the results like – getting rid of *adharmas*, benefitting with all types of wealth and protection from danger.

8. *Twaritā*;

She blesses us holding a noose, a goad and no fear and boon signets in hands. She wears a snake as a jewel. She has a peacock feather in her head. She is always with a group of bears and lions.

This *Devi's Gāyatrī – Om Twaritāyai Ca Vidmahe Mahānityāyai Ca Dīmahe Tanno Nityā Pracodayāt.*

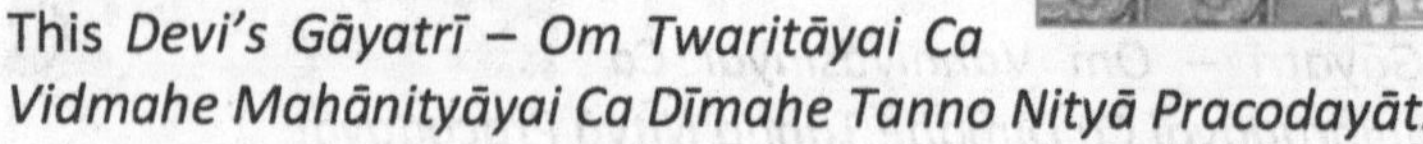

By worshipping this *Devi*, the devotees get the results like – education, knowledge, wealth and health.

9. *Kulasundarī*;

Her image is a peculiar form. She has 6 faces and 12 hands. She holds a book, coral garland, a stylus, a conch and knowledge and boon signets in hands. She is red in colour and has a young moon on the forehead.

This *Devi's Gāyatrī – Om Kulasundaryai Ca Vidmahe Kāmeśvaryai Ca Dīmahe Tanno Nityā Pracodayāt.*

By worshipping this *Devi*, the devotees get the results like – expertise in speech, knowledge, wealth and surrendering of enemies.

10. *Nityā*;

She has 6 faces and 12 hands. Her colour is that of a rising Sun. She holds a goose, goad, sugarcane bow, shield, trident, flower arrow, knife, a skull, book and no fear and boon signets in hands.

This *Devi's Gāyatrī – Om Nitya Bharaivyai Ca Vidmahe Nitya Nityāyai Ca Dīmahe Tanno Nityā Pracodayāt.*

By worshipping this *Devi*, the devotees get the results like – strength of the body and soul and all the eight *Siddhis*.

11. *Nīlapatākā*;

She has 5 faces and 10 hands. Her colour is Blue. She has three eyes. She holds no fear and boon signets in hands. She sits on a lotus flower.

This *Devi's Gāyatrī – Om Nīlapatākāyai Ca Vidmahe Mahā Nityāyai Ca Dīmahe Tanno Nityā Pracodayāt.*

By worshipping this *Devi*, the devotees get the results like – success in examinations and law related issues.

12. *Vijayā*;
She has 5 faces and 10 hands. Her colour is that of a rising Sun. She is surrounded by various other *śaktis*.

This *Devi's Gāyatrī – Om Vijayādevyai Ca Vidmahe Mahā Nityāyai Ca Dīmahe Tanno Nityā Pracodayāt.*

By worshipping this *Devi*, the devotees get the results like – success in battles/ wars, success in arguments, every type of wealth and pride.

13. *Sarvamaṅgalā*;

She is in golden colour. She has three eyes. The Sun and the Moon are her eyes. She sits on a lotus form *Padmāsanā*.

This *Devi's Gāyatrī – Om Svom Om Sarvamaṅgalāyai Ca Vidmahe Chandrādityai Ca Dīmahe Tanno Nityā Pracodayāt.*

By worshipping this *Devi*, the devotees get the results like – knowledge, wealth, successful travels and all auspiciousness.

14. *Jvālāmālinī*;

She has 6 faces, 12 hands and three eyes in each face.

This *Devi's Gāyatrī – Om Jvālāmālāyai Ca Vidmahe Jvālāmālinyai Ca Dīmahe Tanno Nityā Pracodayāt.*

By worshipping this *Devi*, the devotees get the results like – attracting everything including wealth and destruction of all sorrows.

15. *Chitrā*;

She has three eyes and in the colour of rising a Sun.

This *Devi's Gāyatrī – Om Vichitrāyai Ca Vidmahe Mahānityāyai Ca Dīmahe Tanno Nityā Pracodayāt.*

By worshipping this *Devi*, the devotees get the results like –all types wealth.

16. *Mahānityā*;

She is *Śrī Lalitā Parameśvarī* called *Śrī Mahā Tripurasundarī*. Also called as *Avyāja Karuṇā Mūrti*. She is surrounded by all the 15 *Titi Nityā Devis*.

This *Devi's mantra* is the very *Pañcadaśī mantra* itself – *Om aim hrīm śrīm aim ka e I la hrīm ha sa ka ha la hrīm sou: sa ka la hrīm.*

By worshipping this *Devi*, the devotees get the results like – all enjoyments.

The sage *Dūrvāsa* was the son of sage *Adri* and *Anusuyā Devi*. *Dattāreya* was his brother. He installed and worshipped *Kāmākśi* at *Kāñcipuram*.

This has been mentioned in a text called *Kāmākṣi Vilāsam*. He authored '*Lalitāstavaratnam*', containing 200 verses. In that text, the 31st verse prays about *Śrī Chakram*. That verse reads;

Śrī Chakram Śruti Mūlakośa Iti Te Samsāra Chakrātmakam
Vikyātam Tatadiṣṭitākṣara Śivajyotir Mayam Sarvata: |
Etan Mantra Mayātmikāpi-raruṇamśrī Sundarībir-vrutam
Madyebhaintava Simhapīṭa Lalitetvam Brahmavidyā Śive ||

The meaning of this verse is – you are in an auspicious form! It is an all known fact that the *chakra* of yours called *Śrī Chakram* is a kind of root for *Vedas* and a curtain kind for the *Praṇava mantra 'Om'*. The auspicious torch of *Pañcadaśākṣarī mantra*, stated there, is spreading everywhere. The *Āvarṇa Devis*, in the form of *Pañcadaśī* are surrounding you. You in Red colour giantly and valiantly sitting on the throne called *Bindu*. You are in the form of *Brahma Vidyā*.

The root for the *Vedas* is the *Praṇava mantra 'Om'*. The three sides of the center triangle of the *Śrī Chakram* are *A*, *U* and *M* – the combination is *Om*. The *Bindu* is in this form. The covering of this is the *Śrī Chakram*.

Śrī Chakra Navāvarṇa Pooja has deep philosophical meanings. Sinking deep into it, is an impossible task for any human being. It was earlier mentioned about the *Kamalāmbā Navāvarṇa Kīrtanās* of Śrī *Muthuswamy Dīkṣitar*, a great *Śrī Vidyā Upāsakar*. Those *Kīrtanās* are filled with root letters (*bījākṣaras*). Even before him, *Ūtthukāḍu Venkata Kavi* also have wrote *Kāmākṣi Navāvarṇa Kīrtanās*. It is possible to perform *Śrī Chakra Navāvarṇa Pooja*, by singing these *Navāvarṇa Kīrtanās* alone and get the equal results.

Let Śrī *Lalitā Parameśvarī* surrounded by *Titi Nityā Devis*, bless all her compassions to all the readers. There is not even an iota of doubt in this.

Kśamā Prārtanā

During the pooja, some errors omissions and commissions, unknowingly, in *mantras*, actions, focus, etc., either through mind or body, might have arose, on account of ignorance or otherwise. The below verses are seeking pardon (*Kśamā* - क्षमा) from *Śrī Devī* for these errors. Of course, this will not include errors/ mistakes knowingly done.

अपराध सहस्राणि क्रियन्तेऽहर्निशं मया ।
दासोऽयमिति मां मत्वा क्षमस्व परमेश्वरि ॥

Aparāda Sahasrāṇi Kriyante Sharniśam Mayā |
Dāso Syamiti Mām Matvā Kśamasva Parameśvari || 1

अपराधशतं कृत्वा जगदम्बेति चोच्चरेत् ।
यां गतिं समवाप्नोति नतांब्रह्मादय: सुरा: ॥

Aparāda Śatam Krutvā Jagadambeti Choccaret |
Yām Gatim Samavāpnoti Natām Brahmādaya: Surā: || 2

सापराधोऽस्मि शरणं प्राप्तस्त्वां जगदम्बिके ।
इदानीमनुकम्प्योऽहं यथेच्छसि तथा कुरु ॥

Sāparādo Ssmi Śaraṇam Prāptas Tvām Jagadampike |
Idānīmanu Kampyo Sha Yatecchasi Tatā Kuru || 3

अज्ञानाद्विस्मृतेभ्रान्त्या यन्न्यूनमधिकं कृतम् ।
तत्सर्वं क्षम्यतां देवि प्रसीद परमेश्वरि ॥

Agjānād Vismruter Brāntyā Yannyūnamadhikam Krutam |
Tatsarvam Kśamyatām Devi Prasīda Parameśvari || 4

गुह्यातिगुह्यगोप्त्री त्वं गृह्माणास्मत्कृतं जपम् ।
सिद्धिर्भवतु मे देवि त्वत्प्रसादात्सुरेश्वरि ॥

Guhyāti Guhya Goptrī Tvam Gruhāṇāsmatkrutam Japam |
Siddhirbavatu Me Devi Tvatprasādāt Sureśvari || 5

स्वस्ति: प्रजाभ्य: परिपालयन्तां न्याय्येन मार्गेण महीं महीशा: ।
गोब्राह्मणेभ्य: शुभमस्तु नित्यं लोका: समस्ता: सुखिनो भवन्तु ॥

Svasti: Prajābya: Paripālayantām Nyāyyena Mārgeṇa Mahīm Mahīṣā: |
Gobrāhmaṇebya: Śubamastu Nityam Lokā: Samastā: Sukino Bavantu ||6

ॐ तत् सत् श्री जगदम्बार्पणमस्तु॥
Om Tat Sat Śrī Jagadambārpaṇamastu ||

*****

Bibliography

I bow to the feet and convey my sincere thanks from the bottom of my heart, to all those who helped in bringing out this book in the fashion it is. Further the below books/ web-sites were also referenced. Sincere thanks are due to the concerned authors also.

#	Book	Author	Publisher
1.	ஸ்ரீ லலிதா ஸஹஸ்ரநாமம்	S. கணபதி சுப்ரமணியன்	ஞான பாஸ்கர சங்கம், சென்னை
2.	*Śrī Lalitā Sahasranāmam*	Dr. Ramamurthy N (the same author)	CBH Publications, Nagercoil
3.	*Śrī Chakra*, An Esoteric Approach		
4.	Power of *Śrī Vidyā*		
5.	ஸ்ரீ லலிதா த்ரிசதி	மும்பை ராமகிருஷ்ணன்	எல்கேளம் பப்ளிகேஷன், சென்னை
6.	ஸ்ரீ வித்யா	அண்ணா	ராமகிருஷ்ணா மடம், சென்னை
7.	ஸ்ரீ வித்யா பூஜா பத்ததி	ப்ரஹ்மஸ்ரீ டி கல்யாண சுந்தரமய்யர்	ஸ்ரீ ப்ரஹ்ம வித்யா ஞானசபா
8.	நன்மையளிக்கும் நன்மந்திரங்களும் அதன் பயன்களும் - ஷண்மத மந்த்ர கோசம்		ஸ்ரீ புவநேச்வரீ அவதூத வித்யாபீடம், புதுக்கோட்டை
9.	http://www.bookofresearch.com/unexplained-mystery-of-oregon-sri-yantra.htm	Web-site	

Other Books of This Author

http://ramamurthy.jaagruti.co.in/

#	Title	Remarks	No. of pages
	Indology Related		
1.	*Śrī Lalitā Sahasranāmam*	English translation of Śrī *Bhāskararāya's Bhāṣyam*	750
2.	Power of *Śrī Vidyā*		80
3.	*Samatā*	An exposition of Similarities in *Lalitā Sahasranāma* with *Soundaryalaharī, Saptaśatī, Viṣṇu Sahasranāma* and *Śrīmad Bhagavad Gīta*	172
4.	*Advaita* in *Shākta*		80
5.	*Śrī Lalitā Triśatī*	300 divine names of the celestial Mother – **English** translation of *Śrī Ādhi Śaṅkara's Bhāṣyam*	193
6.	Secrets of *Mahāśakti*	Chandi demystified	78
7.	*Daśa Mahā Vidyā*	Ten cosmic forms of the Divine mother	75
8.	ஸ்ரீவித்யா பேதங்கள்	ஸ்ரீவித்யா உபாசனையின் படிகள் - கோவை ஸுதச் சண்டி மலர்	51
9.	ஸ்ரீ தேவீ ஸ்துதிகள்	பல முக்கிய அம்பாள் ஸ்தோத்ரங்கள்	133
10	ஷண்மத மந்த்ரங்கள்	பொள்ளாச்சி ஸ்ரீ ஸஹஸ்ரசண்டி மஹாயாக நினைவு மலர்	145
11	தேவதா மந்த்ரங்கள்	Akkaraipatti Sahasra Chandi Malar	32
12.	ஆதி ஸாங்கரரும் ஷண்மதமும்		32
13	ஸ்ரீ ஷண்மத தேவதா அர்ச்சனை	ஸ்ரீ மஹா கும்பாபிஷேக மலர்	64
14	*Vaidhīka* Wedding	Typical Wedding process in English	56
15	வைதீகத் திருமணம்	Typical Wedding process in Tamil	57
16	ஸ்ரீ லலிதா திரிஸுதி	300 divine names of the celestial Mother – Tamil translation of *Śrī Ādhi Śaṅkara's Bhāṣyam*	234
17	ஸ்ரீகுரு பாதுகா பூஜா விதானம்	சித்தகிரி ஸஹஸ்ரசண்டி மலர்	44
18	ஸ்ரீவித்யா ஸுடாம்னாய மந்த்ரங்கள்	சித்தகிரி ஸஹஸ்ரசண்டி மலர்	60
19	*Ekatā*	Oneness among Shiva, Vishnu and Shakti	277
20	*Vedas* – An Analytical Perspective	A description of Veda, Vedanta, Vedanga, Jyotisha, Shastra, etc.	240
21	*Ṣaṇmata Mantras* – षण्मत मन्त्रा:	Various mantras on Shanmata Gods/ Goddesses	86
22	*Śrīvidya* Variances	Variances in Srividya Upasana	50

#	Title	Remarks	No. of pages
23	வேதங்கள் – ஒரு பகுப்பாய்வு	A description of Veda, Vedanta, Vedanga, Jyotisha, Shastra, etc.	280
24	பரமாச்சார்யாள் நோக்கில் ஸ்ரீலலிதாம்பிகா	The explanation given by Paramacharya on some of the names in Lalita Sahasranama	175
25	*Saṇṇavati* (षण्णवतिः) *Tarpaṇa*	Repaying Debts to Ancestors	42
26	ஷண்ணவதி (षण्णवतिः) தர்ப்பணம்	முன்னோர் கடன் தீர்த்தல்	48
27	*Śrī Mahā Pratyangirā Devī*	Holy Divine mother in ferocious form	41
28	ஸ்ரீ மஹா ப்ரத்யங்கிரா தேவீ	தெய்வீக அன்னையின் பயங்கர வடிவம்	51
29	ஸ்ரீ சக்ர நவாவர்ணம்	ஸ்ரீ சக்ரத்தின் அதிசயங்கள் - கணித, ஆன்மீக, தத்துவ கோணங்களில், ஸ்ரீ சக்ரத்தின் விளக்கம். நவாவரண கோணத்தில் முக்கியத்துவம்.	130
30	*Śrī Chakra Navāvarṇam*	Marvels of *Śrī Chakra* – Perspective of *Śrī Chakra* in Mathematics, philosophy and spiritual angles, with specific reference to *NavĀvarṇam*.	
Applied Samskrutam Based			
31	*Paribhāṣā Stora–s*	An exploration of *Lalitā Sahasranāma*	96
32	*Śrī Chakra*, An Esoteric Approach	Mathematical Construction to draw *Śrī Chakra*	64
33	Number System in Samskrutam		123
34	*Vedic* Mathematics	30 formulae elucidated	146
35	Vedic IT	Information Technology and Samskrutam	162
IT Based			
36	Orthogonal Array	A Statistical Tool for Software Testing	180
Banking Based			
37	Retail Banking		213
38	Corporate Banking		232
39	Dictionary of Financial Terms		215

More books are in pipeline.

Let *Śrī Devī* shower **her** complete compassion on him to share his experiences with others.

Om Tat Sat – ॐ तत् सत्

*****